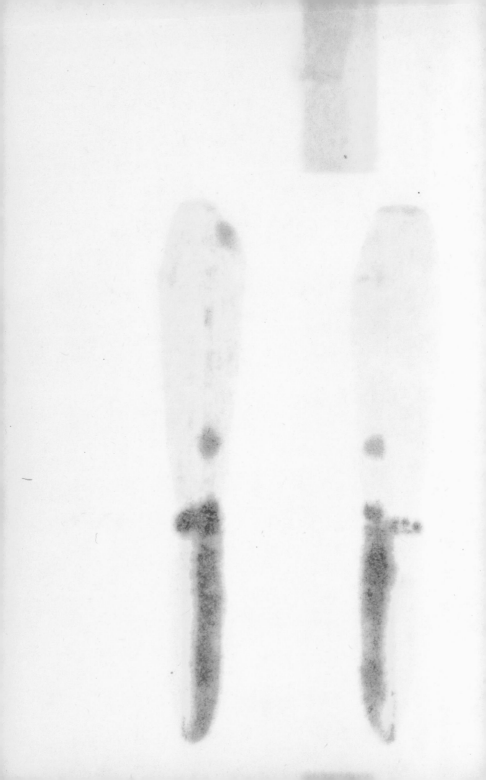

WHAT'S
HAPPENING
TO
AMERICAN
ENGLISH?

WHAT'S HAPPENING TO AMERICAN ENGLISH?

by

Arn Tibbetts
Charlene Tibbetts

☆ ☆

Charles Scribner's Sons ☆ New York

Copyright © 1978 Arnold M. Tibbetts and Charlene Tibbetts

Library of Congress Cataloging in Publication Data

Tibbetts, A. M.
   What's happening to American English?

   1. English language in the United States.
   2. English language—Study and teaching (Secondary)
   3. English language—20th century—Grammar.
   I. Tibbetts, Charlene, joint author.   II. Title.
   PE2807.T5   420'.973   78-10349
   ISBN 0-684-15982-1

1 3 5 7 9 11 13 15 17 19 V/C 20 18 16 14 12 10 8 6 4 2

Printed in the United States of America

To our children—

Susan
Alice
John
Caroline

Contents

Tongues, like governments, have a natural tendency to degeneration; we have long preserved our constitution, let us make some struggles for our language.

—Samuel Johnson, Preface to his *Dictionary* (1755)

Preface

At no time in history has there been so much discussion of the problems with American English. Linguistic experts, teachers at various levels of the educational system, journalists, editors, professional writers, parents, and plain citizens—all have had their say in the matter. While many of the opinions expressed are valuable, one senses a disunity in the arguments put forth. Americans share a common language, yet their points of view, attitudes, and even their training in English now vary so much that they have difficulty finding a common ground.

We hope that we can help to define this ground by taking a fresh look at certain questions: Why is American English in difficulty? What are some of the causes of that difficulty? How are students being taught—or not taught—to speak and write? How can grammar be learned more efficiently? Why are English programs in schools in such confusion? Where have the many bad ideas about language, usage, and pedagogy come from? What can the parent, teacher, and citizen do to improve the situation?

Our answers, of course, will be incomplete and in some instances tentative. Furthermore, they are designed for the general reader rather than for the specialist in linguistics or pedagogy. The specialist customarily distrusts the view of any "nonprofessionals" who may trespass upon a territory he considers his own. We believe that the language belongs to the mass of people who live and die using it, and who have rights in it that even the grammarian, linguist, or lexicographer must acknowledge.

We have our own specialist bias, having taught for many years in American schools. Lumping our experiences together, we have taught in six high schools and junior highs and five colleges and universities, in a total of six states. The high schools ranged from a big-city slum school to a selected-enrollment college-prep school; the colleges, from a third-rate state college to Vanderbilt University. We both have had some teaching experience in high school and college. At the University of Illinois, Arn now teaches grammar and composition to undergraduates about to embark on a teaching career. He is also director of the composition program. Charlene is a curriculum specialist at the university, training graduate students and teaching English to youngsters aged from eleven to seventeen in the "lab school"—the university's experimental school. We have published several composition textbooks for high school and college.

We do not consider ourselves either liberal or conservative in language matters, but realists for whom subjects and verbs ordinarily agree. If we are influenced by any group, it is by historical scholars in English; by any practitioners, the great users of English from Chaucer to Churchill; by any individuals, George Orwell and Samuel Johnson. Our attitudes toward the language are further shaped by more than two half-centuries of using it in a real America, where—in a dozen states—one or the other of us has worked as waitress, office manager, laborer, engineer, teacher, editor, professional writer. We come from country families shaped by the Great Depression: professors we now are, but American peasants we always will be.

The obligations we have incurred in writing this book are too many to list in full. Let us mention the English departments of Vanderbilt University and Peabody College. The

University of Illinois granted the sabbatical leave during which much of the research for the book was done. We are grateful for the support of the university in this and other ways. To the many public school administrators and teachers who spent their valuable time discussing school programs with us, we owe a debt of appreciation and respect. Thanks are also due to the National Council of Teachers of English for allowing us to use portions, somewhat rewritten, of two articles originally published in *The English Journal*.

For encouragement, we owe a debt to Mary Hoag, George Douglas, James Raths, Richard Schreck, Alan Purves, Warren Royer, Anthony Gregorc, Vic Olson, Herschel Gower, James McCrimmon, Frank Moake, Harris Wilson, Francis Weeks, and Peter Givler. Without the advice of Professor John Aden of Vanderbilt University, who ordered us to begin without delay and told us how to proceed, the book would not have been written. Without the help of Jacques Barzun—as great an editor as a writer—the book could not have been published. To him we owe the greatest debt of all.

Arn Tibbetts
Charlene Tibbetts
Urbana, Illinois
January, 1978

WHAT'S HAPPENING TO AMERICAN ENGLISH?

1☆
Beyond Language

We were sitting in the reception room of the hospital, waiting for news. A dear friend was undergoing an operation for cancer. Hoping to turn our thoughts away from the anxiety that clutches one at such times, we divided up a pile of magazines and newspapers that lay on a chair nearby. After a bit we started trading comments:

"Look at this headline: 'ENGINEER JOBS ARE BEGGING FOR WOMEN GRADS.' "

"Here's a drama critic who believes that at the end of its first year, a play is 'both *alive* and *vital*.' "

We collect horrors of this kind: nouns turned into adjectives, as when *engineering* jobs become *engineer* jobs, while the job itself puts on tattered clothes of metaphor and goes *begging;* redundancies which tell the reader that a dramatic production is *alive* and *alive*. Will its second vitality keep it going a second year, after which it will close and close?

Writing, like reading, dispels anxiety, so as we glanced through magazines and newspapers, we took notes for our collection of battered words. In a letter to *Popular Mechanics*, a Chevrolet service manager wrote of a "common taillight outage problem." Then, in another journal, a psychiatrist observed that some unfortunate's "letdown had been very high." In a woman's magazine, a school superintendent described "zero-defect philosophy," which is apparently contaminating the nation's schools. In the advertising section of our hometown paper, there was the announcement of a new business catering to young ladies; it was described as a "dance education facility." And a magazine columnist warned his readers that "you had better take up the job of *parenting* your kids."

In the corner of the reception room, the television set was mumbling quietly to itself. A youngster of about five turned up the sound and then squatted intently in front of it. Two good-looking women commentators were discussing someone whose death required consideration:

"She had a lot of longevity."

"Yes, when you live that long, it's almost like a syndrome."

One of the women interviewed a medical man, who stated that "epidemiologists must expand their expertise." After a moment, the news flashed on, supplying another note for our collection, this time from a policeman: "The maternal parent was placed under surveillance at her home after a report was received that a five-year-old child was in possession of an unknown drug substance."

The doctor we were waiting for finally appeared, still in his medical uniform, swathed in what seemed to be light blue pillow covers. He said something about "a carcinoma in situ." Through the medium of his adopted tongue we discussed the future of the person about whom we were anxious. She would be well and, with luck, live out her years, although the doctor declined to state his opinion in the common language of our ancestors.

That common language is disappearing. It is slowly being crushed to death under the weight of a verbal conglomerate, a pseudospeech at once pretentious and feeble, that is created daily by millions of blunders and inaccuracies in grammar, syntax, idiom, metaphor, logic, and common sense. Merely to glance at the scribbled lists we carried out of the hospital invites both wonder and dismay. When a journalist writes that *jobs beg* for graduates and a psychiatrist sees nothing funny in a *high letdown,* we may infer that about thirty-five years of education can teach two professional men nothing about metaphor—or its dangers. Our columnist, who is paid to use the English language, does not know that *parenting* is as impossible as *childing,* nor can our attractive university graduates on television separate genuine idiom from nonsense. It would indeed be syndromic to have *a lot of longevity*—less so, perhaps, to have a lot of training in English.

Even more alarming are the crushing effects of this verbal conglomerate as it is employed by what used to be known as "the common man." Hardly precious in style or outlook, generally uneducated in either the better or worse senses of the term, the common man of only three generations ago could ordinarily be depended upon to go his ungrammatical way and still make himself understood. "It ain't fitten," said Arn's grandfather on occasion. It was claimed that he could read, but few relatives could be found who had actually seen him do it. And he never wrote. Yet his speech was as clear and natural as the spring water that was piped by gravity into a large barrel in the corner of his farm kitchen. Grandfather repaired his own machinery and would have said, "The tail light is out on the T Ford." (It was always *T Ford,* never *Model T.*) Today, his great-grandson might find nothing strange in a constipated nounal abstract like *taillight outage problem;* while his great-granddaughter, similarly afflicted by modern nonidiom, would advertise her *dance education facility.* Until recently, conversation like this, recorded during a radio interview, was impossible:

"We will take economic action!" said the worker.
"What?" said the interviewer.
"There will be a viable move towards intervention!"
"What?"
"Strike!"

5

As the modern researcher is likely to say, "We do not have an insufficient data base." These characteristic ways of not coming out with the idea but of roaming jargonistically around it are choking the life out of English and destroying the ability to think in the peoples that used to speak that wonderfully expressive tongue. Illustrations of the verbal pollution are all around us. A sign in Yosemite National Park: "Bear Habitat." The secretary of the treasury proposes, as one way of reforming estate taxes, a device called "free interspousal transfer." Fortunately, a senator at the hearing catches him up: "You mean wife-swapping?"

The distortions of American English we have been quoting do not as a rule represent normal change or dialectal variation as these are recorded by scholars. Nor are they the result of too little formal education; the worst offenses are found in the writing of the "educated," as in this passage from a bylined story on the front page of a major newspaper: "Everything was coming up roses for a young west suburban married couple as long as two pay-checks—his and hers—were rolling in. Then came the first of five children. And the cozy little two-paycheck dream world of Donald B. and his wife, Phyllis, collapsed into a rat race—slowly at first. Then the vicious circle of debt accumulation began to close in. When its grip was total, it embraced the young couple in $5,000 worth of debts." It is significant that university English majors preparing to teach usually do not see anything strange in that passage. Nor, apparently, did the writer who shifts through metaphors involving *roses, rolling in, dream world, rat race,* and a *vicious circle* that closes, grips, and embraces.*

---

* Incompetence in handling metaphor can now be found even in the best edited of modern journals: "If he were trying to pull himself together by hanging on to Esther's sanity, and she knew that and parlayed it, there would be some dynamics, and some edges. The vacuum in this movie is the purity of their relationship. John Norman catapults her to success without her knowing what his plans for her are. . . ."—*The New Yorker*

One of the problems in writing about the new pseudo-English lies in finding the right nomenclature. Terms like *jargon, gobbledygook, cant, argot,* and so on have their uses; but they apply poorly here, partly because the new "English" covers all of these and more and partly because there is something nonlinguistic and inhuman about it.

In 1958, Willard Thorp (then chairman of the English Department at Princeton) remarked on "a sinister change in the kind of writing we have lately been getting from our students. . . . We are now too often presented with a kind of prose—if that is the name for it—which is inviolable. A red-pencil used against it becomes as impotent as a sword in a folk-tale which has had a spell put on it. Sometimes this prose resembles remotely a bad translation from a foreign language. Sometimes it suggests that the writer has squeezed together under pressure the jagged ends of several assorted ideas."[1] The implication here is that we are faced with something outside the normal experience of English speakers. Far from being a result of normal linguistic change, our verbal monster represents language as it might be seen in one of those wavy mirrors at a fun house, in which the reflected grotesqueries of one's image are changed from second to second as one approaches it, each new image weirder and less recognizable than the last. We will call this apparition *Unspeech,* an expression as awkward and shapeless as the thing itself.

Unspeech came slowly into being after World War II, when a unified rhetoric based on reason was giving way to persuasions of another kind. Rock music, for example, employs language; but given the amplification of the music, you cannot hear or understand the words, nor are you supposed to. The English of the Nixon administration was meant to be heard but not fully understood, since it was at once a private code and a set of misleading signals to the public. Both of these examples (and many others are available) point to a significant use of Unspeech—as camouflage for the real business at hand. At the enormous yearly meetings of the Modern Language Association (MLA), few professors listen to the papers (they are not designed for the ear anyhow), which are no more than a necessary accompaniment to the real political and social business of conventioneering.

But hasn't this always been so? Haven't the empty social forms always tended to prevail over general content? To some extent, yes. But in the history of modern English there is no period in which such victory over thought-in-speech has been so widespread. Nor in the past has the general idiom, on which we depend for our very understanding of vital matters, been so seriously distorted. And, of course, linguistic distortions help to create rhetorical ones. We have been told by an expert editor of medical literature that articles are now being published in prestigious medical journals in which the evidence presented bears few logical, rhetorical, or scientific connections to either the author's thesis or conclusions. "Then why," we asked, "are these articles accepted? Why don't the editors and the authorities who must pass on the article in question turn down such stuff?" Because, the expert answered, "much medical publishing is empty exercise—no one *expects* genuine connections to be made."

At one time Arn served as a technical editor. Part of his job was to remove nonsense and ambiguity from books on a variety of subjects, ranging from engineering to geopolitics. This sort of work is found increasingly necessary in publishing houses and scientific journals, a sign that our most highly trained minds can no longer write up their own findings. Once, in a four-volume series on airplanes written for technicians, Arn found a section in the fourth volume that was a word-for-word repetition of material in the second. The series had already undergone editing twice. What had happened was that the jargon of Unspeech had so successfully narcotized the previous readers' minds that four authors and two editors had failed to recognize ten pages of repetition. Since those pages said nothing anyway, they were cut without loss. It is typical of modern prose that one can chop large chunks of it out and never miss them. Indeed, thorough editing may eliminate a project: too little is left to make a book.

Before attempting to give an account of the nature, forms, and causes of the false tongue now replacing English, let us say a few words about the notorious example of it that reached the public through the Watergate hearings. For months, while the scandal was unfolding, the press had a pleasant time ridiculing the jargon that befogged the testimony—*plumbers, time frame, office facility* (applied to a person), *deny-ability, zero-defect system.* Yet there was more to the language of Watergate than the incompetence of politicians whose mismatched vocables showed incoherent thought. Everybody involved—the investigators and the investigated—disclosed their illiteracy, or at least their habitual fumbling with American English. Mispronunciations, faulty agreements, ambiguous referents, foggier-than-thou abstractions, wild metaphors, sentences that started and ended in syntactic confusion—all were freely displayed to the viewer-listener. One got the impression from these American leaders, many of them products of our best universities, that to them English was a foreign language imperfectly learned.

Watergate speech is significant as the clear symptom of a general disease. The Watergaters spoke and wrote much as many "educated" Americans have been speaking and writing for some time. If this seems an exaggeration, here are two examples of "educated" usage: (1) "Substantial accomplishments were put under people's belts before the bloom began to fade" (an authority on pollution, 1975). (2) "The social systems which organize and rationalize contemporary life have always been ingeniously armed for the day when youth

9

would rebel against the essentially pastoral status assigned to it" (the head of the English department in a leading university, 1968).[2]

Number 2 above is the first sentence in a lead article in *The Atlantic Monthly*, and it is typical of the article as a whole. One wants to ask how a system, being inert, can *organize* or *rationalize* anything or be *ingeniously armed;* how a reader is to find out what *pastoral status* means; and what the author intends the terminal *it* to refer to—*life, day, youth, status?*

In a word, we reached the point ten years ago where the editor of a leading American magazine, an old and honorable journal of opinion, felt no embarrassment at publishing undecipherable jargon. How did we get to this point? What are the causes of our predicament? "Cause" in cultural matters is always difficult to ascertain. One often has to be content with partial correlations; and it is generally true that cause and effect play hide and seek, the effect becoming a cause in its turn.

One clear cause, certainly, can be found in our American passion for social leveling. Language is intimately bound up with social life. Consider the auto mechanic who is also a father, a member of the American Legion, a Democrat, a school-board member, and a Methodist. He is each of these to the extent that he can use the language expected in these several roles. He cannot repair a car, work effectively for his political party, or object to the new wing being planned for his church without using some brand of American English. And our mechanic, if he is typically American, is ostentatiously a leveler. He is as good as anybody else, and nobody else is better than he. While he looks up to men who have certain kinds of knowledge that he considers arcane, such as the knowledge of how the stock market works, the tendency of his social beliefs is toward equality. And he uses every device at his disposal to gain such equality. The average

American is never happier than when he can, through taxes, soak the rich, or, through revisions of the law, keep millions of equal children in the educational system who might—if they had free choice—cheerfully leave school for the pleasures of work.

Now we ourselves do not object, at least in theory, to the sociopolitical desires of the mechanic. Considering our modest means, soaking the rich looks like fun. These remarks on leveling are made without bias and in a sad scientific spirit, as H. L. Mencken might say. Like the mechanic, we believe in education. In fact, we are hardly different from him in our prejudices. Yet it must be admitted that, to take only an educational example, a nationwide school system full of unhappy children, some of whom regularly carry weapons, does not produce "quality education."

The cliché just embraced with quotation marks represents some of the effect that social leveling has had on the American language. To the leveler, words—like people—are all equal. Distinctions tend to disappear; the very idea of them is uncongenial. At the same time, terms and phrases in common use must sound complimentary and luxurious, as in advertising—thus, expressions like *quality education,* heard on the same day from the chief mechanic at the local Pontiac dealer and on television from the governor of the state. What is wrong here is that the phrase means everything and nothing. It is spherical and can roll in any direction.

Such phrases have become common because they suit the leveling spirit by flattering everybody, every school, every student without distinction—or definition—of meanings. The double result is that the language and thought of those using such terms lose more and more their sharpness, precision, force—in short, become characterless.

One of the ablest American academic linguists, the late Albert Marckwardt, wrote in 1966: "Much of the country lacks a critical ear and a cultivated voice, and indeed it feels—mistakenly, of course—that it is somehow democratic to be this way." Marckwardt also told of a scholar from the University of London who came to the United States to lecture. According to this scholar, the only "assured speakers" of English she found were "two old ladies in Charleston, South Carolina."[3] Perhaps their assurance came from the feeling that they did not have to prove to others their democratic connections, their desire to be "with it," or their preference for the latest expression in vogue.

It has been asserted by certain modern linguists that American English has not been declining in this century. We will analyze their premises in some detail in Chapter Four. The evidence, it seems, leads to a different conclusion. One can search through the annals of our nineteenth century and find ordinary communications—those of politicians excepted—generally free of verbal pollution. Here, for example, is a letter written a century ago by a Nebraska gentleman of some importance to a physician of his acquaintance:

> Dear Doc,
>
> If you are alive or dead for God's sake let me know as this is the third time I have written you, but still no answer. It may be on account of the wandering life we lead your letters have miscarried. We moved from Kearney to Platte City, stayed there a month and shoved out for this point from whence we expect to be routed ere the next moon. When I came here a month ago Julesburg was no bigger than a portable bean box. Now it contains some 3 or 4 hundred houses, mostly saloons and restaurants well seasoned with gamblers, whores and whore houses. I verily believe that all those wretched cusses who are happily destined to line the road to Hell when that awful day arrives are collected here. You are losing greenbacks by your absence from this delectable hell. In a few weeks clap will be a specialty thick enough to dig off

with a shovel. You could not scare up an uglier set of old whores, no, not even in Mexico. Business is lively. Freeman is here printing his Index. I paid him the amount of your indebtedness, so soon as I hear from you I will remit. Hoping you are well and doing well, I am yours &c.

John Siddell[4]

Sixteen years later, the physician thus addressed was a successful doctor in Colorado. He wrote to a woman in Denver this answer about her tubercular husband:

My advice is short, but I know it is good. Tell him to dismiss all thoughts of curing his lungs; it can't be done, never could be, never will be by way of lung remedies. Nature will cure them if she can. No doctor can. This is the dark side of the picture. Now for the bright: most consumptives die because they depend on lung remedies. Many get well, but usually because they have quit the use of lung remedies. If your husband has had consumption long he knows that when his appetite and digestion are good he gets better (his lungs, too) and that whenever his digestion fails his lungs get worse. That is the whole secret. Now let him profit by his own knowledge obtained in his own experience. . . .[5]

One of these writers was, by the standard of the time, an educated man. He may or may not have thought of himself as above the common ranks. But the interesting fact is that despite their status and without false dignity, both men used the language as "assured speakers," vividly and precisely, without a trace of the pedantry, abstraction, incompetent metaphor, and cluttered syntax that we find today among people with much more "schooling" than these and other nineteenth-century Americans enjoyed. If a doctor today wrote so clear a letter on a medical problem, he would be regarded with suspicion, and if the less polished author of the first letter were judged by its form and contents, he

13

might be (mistakenly) marked down as a poor writer, because it is clear and direct.

As individuals, we Americans are becoming more interchangeable, like the parts of a machine. Accordingly, our language is becoming more featureless amd machinelike, with its parts—as George Orwell definitively put it—consisting "less and less of *words* chosen for the sake of their meaning, and more and more of *phrases* tacked together like the sections of a prefabricated hen-house."[6] Prefab Unspeech is now a leading mode of communication. You can say *concept of the Communist conspiracy* in one breath and *concept of garbage collection* in another, and nobody will blink an eye. We took our daughter to an expensive dental surgeon, and he remarked, "An operation is not contraindicated." A doctor of education wrote to Arn about a test he had given to a part of his class: "This data in order to be validated should be administrated in terms of the whole class of your testees." Arn decided to leave them unadministrated, the thing sounded so painful.

If prefab Unspeech were used by a certain, easily identifiable group of natives, there would be less cause for dismay. One might conceivably declare war on it and even get help from the agencies that protect consumers, and that would be that. But the corruption afflicts nearly the entire population, from the drugstore owner to the college president. Even some of our creative writers have caught the disease, as Katherine Anne Porter implied when she said, "So many words that had good meanings once upon a time have come to have meanings almost evil—certainly shabby, certainly inaccurate. And 'psychology' is one of them. It has been so abused. . . . too many of the young writers have got so soaked in the Freudian and post-Freudian vocabulary that they can't speak—not only can't speak English, but they can't speak *any* human language any more."[7]

In some circles an active attack on our human language is

taking place, resulting in what might be called verbicide. Consider the murder of such fine old words as *man* and *lady*, to mention only two examples. In some areas of intellectual life, *man* has been buried alive. After the chancellor of a university officially outlawed its use in words like *chairman*, *chairpersons* blossomed forth in the faculty directory. And, in another realm, what virile *gentleperson* would dare to say, "I was feeling *gay* at the party last night"? Killing off words for one arbitrary reason or another neuters the human being while clamping him/her/it in the iron vise of ideology. Hortense Calisher, the novelist, complains, "I find myself now responsible to a whole Ms-ship of assumptions—just as I now answer socially to a syllable which sounds like a bumblebee breaking wind, where before I enjoyed the truly equal form of address, my name."[8]

Another cause of our linguistic depletion is the incessantly growing number of technical specialties, many of them theoretical, some very speculative, others imaginary and pretentious. It would take a full page just to list the subspecialties that have appeared in the last quarter-century in the subject under discussion, grammar and rhetoric. The more theoretical the discipline, the more it tends to split into new "fields," which exist largely thanks to their own jargon. Imagine the grantsmanship one can carry on by using a phrase like *social ecology*.

When Arn worked in the oil fields before going into academic life, the older geologists often referred in their written reports to *lows*. A *low*—the vernacular term for a subsurface depression in the rock beds—could be *short, long, narrow, wide,* and so on. As self-conscious young geologists from the universities joined the profession, one began to hear more of *synclines* (*geosynclines,* if they were large). Still later, the newest graduates were threatening the universe with expressions like *orthogeosynclines.* This example can be matched again and again.

Everything we Americans do or think about has been turned into a hothouse for nomenclature. We have a passion for classifying. Rhetoric itself has been invaded by the tax-onomical mind, so that now teachers of language are expected to use words like *metarhetoric, diachronic, programmatic*. Taxonomy, classification and its terms, is useful in the natural world. Of the roughly ten million species (plants and animals) on earth, scientists have classified 10 to 15 percent. But as Patrick Ryan observed, taxonomists

> tend to finish up knowing more about the intricacies of the system of classification than they do about the living things they're classifying. The extent of this paradox may be judged from the current use by some schools of stratification of up to 21 levels of hierarchy in the classification of any large group of mammals. Thus, for example, the complete taxonomic identification of your pet dog would require 19 levels of description from Kingdom Animalia, Subkingdom Metazoa, Phylum Chordata, Subphylum Vertebrata . . . and so on down through a dozen more rankings to Genus *Canis,* Subgenus (none) and finally Species *Canis familiaris*. I am by nature the last chap to carp at a taxonomist, but it does seem a bit extravagant to use 19 levels, 39 words, and around 300 letters to come up with the fact that what's just bitten you is undubitably a three-letter word, dog. [9]

The rejoinder when objections are made to words like *metarhetoric, ruggedize, marital deviance*, and *preprint* is that they are a necessary part of "our technical language." But is this true? Who gains and who loses when the man who runs a car-wash and a ladies' hairdresser each begin to speak in newfangled technical language? All they can talk to each other about is the weather—and even the possibility of rain masquerades as *precipitation probability*.

Persons who operate a car-wash, set women's hair, teach composition, fly rockets, determine economic policy, or try to keep their neighbors from going out of their minds do not in fact need a set of agglutinating technical terms to sub-subclassify the commonplace facts and actions that make up their daily chores. Just as a geologist was once able to write a report using simple words like *high* and *low*, a professor can still write a critical piece on satire without *satura*, *persona*, *eiron*, and *burla*. The famous literary scholar Douglas Bush maintained that "the most precise and subtle ideas about literature can be expressed in ordinary language."[10] It seems likely that the "precise and subtle ideas" about almost any subject now need as much ordinary language as possible.

Not only scientists, but business and professional men today have yet to learn—or rather to remember—this fundamental idea: to be excessively precise in classification is to tinker with the truth. Their terminology is more clear-cut than reality. They tend to deceive themselves as they putter about a problem carrying all those shiny pieces of verbal equipment, most of which cannot be used either to analyze the situation accurately or to explain it to others. In his *Social Sciences as Sorcery*, Stanislav Andreski remarks how the language of social science often deceives or, at the very least—as he puts it in his analysis of a well-known sociologist's theory of action—results in "incredibly ponderous restatements of the obvious."[11]

Americans are uncomfortable about many aspects of their lives unless they can explain them with some theory or verbal scheme. Even housewives wield terms like *detergent pollutant* as easily as they wield a mop. Yet theories do not have to be mainly true or even conform mainly to reality. Excepting the hard sciences, the typical modern theory exists as little more than a taxonomic verbalization. The mathematician Hao Wang comments on this point:

> In order to evaluate the theory, you have first to understand it. In order to understand it, you have first to learn a new

language. Since it is usually impossible to explain clearly and exactly even the technical usages, a formal or exact theory can almost always be defended against charges that it does not conform to fact. As long as there is a sufficiently complicated system and a fairly big and energetic group of people who, for one reason or another, enjoy elaborating the system, we have a powerful school of learning, be it the theory of meaning, the sociology of knowledge, or the logic of induction. There is always the hope that further development of the theory will yield keys to old puzzles or fertilise the spirit of new invention. In any case, since there is mutual support between different parts of a given system, there is little danger that the discrepancy between one part and the facts should discredit the system. And of course if we are interested in the "foundations," there is no need to fear any immediate tests. The worst that can happen to such theories is not refutation but neglect.[12]

Hao Wang's final remark applies with particular force to many American-made theories both in and out of science, especially those about education. Although they are endlessly discussed, such theories are not ordinarily refuted in newspapers, magazines, or television. They just fade away, only to be revived in a decade or two under another name. In the past half-century, what was originally known as "progressive education" has had at least two careers and may have one or two more before the end of the century.

While the faddism of technical jargons may not influence all Americans, fad words in the general language do. They make up another cause of the present corruption of speech. Faddism in so-called standard English used to be relatively unimportant, involving the verbal toys of idle, ignorant, or childish people. Usually it did not matter what they said. Like the wordplay of adolescents, fad language had small influence on what mature and civilized persons thought or did.

But in recent years the situation has changed in three fundamental ways. First, there is a tendency toward treating all opinions as equal. They need not be sensible, well put, or coherent. Degrees of authority are hardly taken into account. As a result, children inform the public that their high school courses do not fit their needs; movie actresses tell us how to conduct wars; illiterate housewives philosophize in letters to the editor about the evils of certain books in the curriculum.

The din of fad words is omnipresent: *detente, quality* ___ (fill in the blank, as in *quality transportation*), *commitment, concept, hopefully, elitist, activist, motivation, relevant, image, credibility gap, interface, module, viable, vital, structured.* As in other fads—of dress, music, literature, cults— the words suddenly appear, give glamour to every other sentence, and then go into partial retirement. Some of the examples given here are already rapidly getting out of date. The analogy between fads in American English and in dress is not farfetched: one both dresses and speaks in particular ways so as to be part of the "now crowd" (the phrase itself is faddish).

Our situation has changed in a second fundamental way. When fad English is uttered, few people today ask, Does it mean anything? We have lost the simple urge to ask, for example, Just what is *quality education* anyway? One popular response to many a remark these days is, *That's a lot of crap.* This verdict is scarcely informative; it points to none of the logical or rhetorical features of articulate utterance; it is only a reaction of dislike, disapproval, possibly of hatred. In contrast, lucid statements are often received with instinctive suspicion. We overheard this exchange in a truck stop:

FIRST TRUCKER: I heard that [a politician] lied to the FBI.
SECOND TRUCKER: What do you mean—uh? What the goddam hell do you mean?
Compared to many political remarks these days, the first

trucker's observation was transparent, and the second trucker was immediately suspicious because he *could* understand it. Had it been put in a fad language, with an "image" here and an "inoperative" there, he might not have had to miss a slurp of his coffee.

A third change in our relation to language has to do with our attitudes toward politics. Whereas sociability used to avoid quarrelsomeness by excluding the political and religious slogans of the day, now almost every part of our lives has been invaded by the verbal fads of politics. A college freshman can write of the *power structure* in his university and of his family. Battles between the second and third sexes bring on cries of *fag* and *straight*. *Honky* and *whitey* are still available to those who wish to make race relations more wretched than they are. Husbands are *sexist* or *chauvinist;* Ah, Nicholas Chauvin, you should be living at this hour! In a cartoon, an overbearing little girl turns out to be a *female chauvinist piglet*. The world is full of *greasers, WASPs, elitists, bourgeois, far-outs, New Lefts*, and *Maoists*, all of them resisting or accepting the labels without clear notions of what they mean.

Our new American condition will not soon change. We are so politicized that practically any issue of interest to human beings is now discussed in the lowest language of governmental power. The best instance is the universal use of the word *right*, with less and less sharpness of meaning attached. A sixteen-year-old boy has a *right* to the family car; that is, he wants it, he claims it, and he tries to make the claim good by improvising a *right*, vested in sixteen-year-olds. "Does the word *right* mean much nowadays?" we asked a university sophomore. "Meaning is crap," he said. "It's what you can get that counts."

The examples so far given of Unspeech will be familiar to anyone who reads and listens today. For those who have professional experience or interest in American English they may carry special poignance. It will be useful to ask two questions: Beyond their mere existence, what do such examples amount to? Can any deeper analysis be made of certain diseases in the language? Those who might be expected to help us most in this endeavor—the philologists and linguists—have little to say. The established academic church tends to frown on investigations of evidence which suggest that linguistic change can be for the worse (see Chapter Four).

The most effective analysis of modern jargon was carried out by George Orwell as a part of his political writing. His letters and essays often contain references to contemporary usages that violate idiom—more, that violate the human being and his sense of reality. Orwell's novels, *Animal Farm* and *1984*, employ as a major theme the remaking of reality through the distortion of language. Since words do (and should) reflect reality, the totalitarian can change the citizen's view of the world by changing his language. In *1984*, the government develops a degraded form of English that Orwell called Newspeak, which was deliberately designed to make truth less accessible to the people.

Newspeak had some characteristics of a genuine language, including a basic vocabulary and a grammar, both seriously debased and made more mechanical for greater control by the dictatorship. What Willard Thorp called No-English and we have termed Unspeech is significantly different from Newspeak in that it has moved beyond language. And in doing so it has added an important trait: it is impenetrable to thought. In one fashion or another, Unspeech defies the very system that allows English to perform its duties of communication.

The elements of this system are many, but two major ones can be mentioned—choice of words (or how words reflect one's sense of reality) and grammar (or how the order and form of words help to create and communicate statements).

Violate either of these elements of system in spoken or written English, and nobody can penetrate your meaning. It is that kind of language which Thorp called inviolable. From a state senator in Georgia: "The smugness of those who have seized the reins of government in the last half decade has resulted in the nullification of the needs of the needy." And witness the complaint of Alan Smith, science attaché of the British Embassy in Washington, commenting on the new Toxic Substances Control Act: "I cannot understand the language of the Act. In its wording, a chemical substance is not a chemical substance; the environment is not the environment; . . . *manufacture* means *import;* in short, everything means everything—including everything else." [13]

Unspeech is made impenetrable by certain distortions of usage and grammar. Let us consider a few.

In a publisher's description of a reputable desk dictionary, we read this sentence: "English teachers everywhere agree that personal ownership and use of a good desk dictionary is a prime necessity for every student in obtaining the maximum results from the study of English." The sentence is badly made, with redundant adjectives, feeble nouns, and a surplus of prepositions. Preposition piling is a fairly good sign of imminent breakdown in thought. To avoid breakdown, we need to rethink the publisher's sentence by picking out certain subjects and verbs: *Teachers* (s) *agree* (v). On what do they agree? That *Students* (s) *should own* (v) *and use* (v) *a good desk dictionary.*

Now that we have by our own efforts pulled out a somewhat clearer idea from the anemic original, we ask: Is the statement true? No. All we can say is: *Most English teachers agree that students should own and use a good desk dictionary.* And with that modification, we see the pointlessness of *prime necessity* and *maximum results:* no dictionary justifies these claims even if they are precisely put.

Before leaving our bedraggled sentence, let us make one more point concerning its grammatical distortion. Solidly made English sentences have a requirement seldom mentioned by grammarians: Sentence statements are best made in precise noun-verb relationships within clauses. It is not true, as so many teachers have told so many students, that the important thing in a sentence is the verb. Rather, one important thing is a relationship: that between a properly chosen noun-subject and its own verb. Clear statements are made through grammatical interaction of subject and verb. In the original sentence, the clause that begins with *ownership* and *use* has nowhere to go; no verb can be found that makes a satisfactory statement.

There is a broad, vague boundary where grammar and usage meet and overlap. The question of agreement in the original sentence (*ownership* and *use is*) involves both grammar and usage, while the carelessness in wording is mainly a matter of usage and, occasionally, of logic and thinking the matter through. It is impossible, for example, that teachers *everywhere* could ever be persuaded to agree on anything. *Personal ownership* is redundant. What does it mean to say that *ownership* or *use* is a *necessity?* There is no useful distinction between a *necessity* and a *prime necessity.* And so on.

In practice, grammar and usage also influence each other. A writer's habit of employing Unspeech softens his grammatical bones—and his mind. What he writes is formless, clumsy, and obese, while at the same time his powers of thought and observation decay. Layers of verbal fat cover the mushy structure of his statements, and the reader has difficulty deciphering the grammatical code. Distinctions among parts of speech become blurred. The editors of *Science* were not embarrassed to publish this: "A major part . . . of the hypothalamus has been lesioned." Francis Straus commented on this passage in the letters column: "Whoever allowed a previously respectable noun to be verbed should be violenced. . . . Good nouns are hard to keep virtuous, and their prostitution should be crimed."[14]

Of course no one should object to "functional shift," as grammarians call it, when it is euphonious, logical, and idiomatic. One can *gravel* (verb) his driveway with *gravel* (noun) and thus have a *gravel* (adjective) drive; but when the *gravel man* (as our children called him) pours pieces of rock over the geraniums, that is not a *gravel mistake.* Idiom is a narrow-minded old lady with a whim of iron.

A good working rule: To avoid linguistic distortion, keep the elements of the grammatical code as clear and firm as possible. A serious violation of this rule is the increasing habit of many writers to make nouns do more grammatical work than they can reasonably perform. Even in context, one can hardly tell what these distortions mean: *adolescence enrichment program, education modality, reaction facility.* The diagnosis is overweening love of nouns, a condition that causes the writer to jam nouns—usually abstract ones— together to form incomprehensible clots.

If anyone questions this generality, let him follow the doubts and difficulties set forth by Bruce Price in an essay which first takes up a book entitled *Reality Therapy:*

> Do you gather that the author uses reality as a means of therapy or that the goal of his treatment is facing reality or that he has worked out some sort of therapy which he applies to reality? Take a phrase puzzled over in *Newsweek:* "antenna television systems operation." Manufacture? broadcasting? consulting? The article said that somebody was going into that field and I still don't know where he's going. I suspect that the people who turn out these phrases might insist that they are seeking greater precision, as though each new noun pinned down the matter a bit more. Wrong. Another article

like this one and we'll have a modifier noun proliferation
increase phenomenon article protest campaign, but will you
know what you've got? [15]

Yet the mumbo-jumbo created by proliferating nouns does
more than merely befuddle. To call a library, in good Unspeech, an *instruction resource center* turns a collection of
books, many of them monuments to the human spirit, into
something mechanical and nonhuman. In his presidential
address to the Linguistic Society of America in 1972, Professor Dwight Bolinger pointed out how important grammatical
devices can be in the act of naming. *He responded to her cry
of distress* is, as Bolinger explained, "at least neutral as
regards sympathy. But in a sentence like *He responded to
her distress cry*, you sense an incongruity. *Distress cry* adds
something to the lexicon; it sets up a classification, and does
it in a clinical way—for observation, not for pity or for
hate." [16] Yet how many of us would now sense the difference
that expressions like *distress cry* can make to us as feeling
persons?

The exchange of ideas is dehumanized by the writer who
with clinical detachment tends to treat in the same way
everything he sees. The bombing raid, the starving children,
the theft of political documents, the drunken wife beater,
the October sunset, the sexual climax—all become abstract
punched-card events in the writer's great Information Re-
trieval Systems Data Bank.

This baleful tendency goes beyond the realm of the noun
as modifier. The noun has invaded the house of predication,
where useful grammatical energies are created. In effective
sentences, predication works like this: "The city council *did
not approve the new stoplight* because the city engineer *said*
he *could not find room for it on the right of way.*" The writer
in thrall to nouns will blot out the predication in the subordinate clauses and successfully hide most of the information in

nouny abstraction: "The city council did not approve the new stoplight because of a *question of feasibility.*" Or again: "*Due to a mechanism unit breakdown,* the photocopy machine is not running this week." "The reason for the vacation being changed is *nonresidence student complaint* concerning time for *examination preparation.*" This last sentence actually says that *reason is complaint.*

Underlying the modern distortions of grammar is a major principle: grammatical function must be obscured.

This can be accomplished in a number of ways. One can wreck predication by separating a subject from its verb, as this lawyer does: "Certainly a congressional *finding* that residence requirements allowed each State to concentrate its resources upon new and increased programs of rehabilitation ultimately resulting in an enhanced flow of commerce as the economic condition of welfare recipients progressively improved *is* rational. . . ."[17] In full, this sentence runs to fifty-one words. Lawyers do not love brevity, a fact which encouraged Chief Justice Warren Burger to growl at a law professor, "You filed a 216-page brief when 75 pages easily would have done it."[18] Yet Justice Burger is himself a sinner. After reading twenty-two opinions of the Court in 1976, James Kilpatrick remarked that the Chief Justice knows not the purpose of a period: "Warren Burger writes a sentence of 65 words as soddenly as he writes a sentence of only 58."[19]

The user of Unspeech is most successful when he can combine several distortions of grammar at the same time. Our example starts, *However, the emotion appeals to us.* . . . This seems clear enough. We easily recognize the subject-verb relation as *emotion appeals.* But the sentence continues, *However, the emotion appeals to us are carefully rationalized.* . . . We got it wrong: *emotion* is supposed to work as an adjective; a noun has been forced to do an adjective's work, and the subject-verb relation is *appeals are rationalized.* But the passive throws us off the track: who is doing the rationalizing? The sentence has further to go: *However, the emotion appeals to us are carefully rationalized, except the crackpot ones, making us responsible persons.* The last phrase, using the *-ing* word *making,* is adjectival. It is a familiar construction, as in *Smiling, the boy fell dead. Smiling* modifies *boy.* But what does *making us responsible persons* modify? The writer keeps such secrets as a matter of taking pride in obscurity.

Here is a more subtle instance of distortion. The writer is a well-known woman novelist and critic, who is writing about Shakespeare's *Macbeth:* "Thus the virtue of having a good conscience is seen by him in terms of bodily hygiene, as if it were a Simmons mattress or an electric blanket." The remark trudges along for twelve words, stumbling over a clumsy passive to make matters a bit awkward, until it gets to *him.* Now the author teeters on the edge of a gap in the sentence. How is she going to get from *him* to *bodily hygiene? Voilà!* She leaps the gap with *in terms of,* leaving the reader perched on the pronoun *him* and wondering where our leader has got to. Since there are no *terms* in the sentence and the light cast by the metaphor is dim indeed, the reader is stuck in the middle of this shaky structure, left to ponder the anachronistic mixture of Shakespeare, Simmons mattresses, electric blankets, bodily hygiene, and Macbeth's conscience. Double, double toil and trouble.

Such are the larger misdeeds of grammatical distortion. Of the smaller ones, we could name and illustrate dozens, but a few examples will suffice:

—*The floating adverb about to sink:* "*Hopefully,* Detroit will win the pennant." "*Regretfully,* the senate failed to pass the bill." Our favorite example of the type: "*Sorrily,* early auto design did not follow engineering."

—*The preposition that attaches itself to any passing verb:* "The President will meet *with* his advisors and counsel *with*

27

them." "Let us sit *in* on this committee" (when the meaning is not "to come as an observer").

—*The half-mad modifier:* "The final pleasure came in eating the fish he caught with fried potatoes, sliced tomatoes, and a can of beer." "The fraternities voted for the queen as a body."

—*The incomparable comparison:* "He says his writing is easier to read than his secretary." "More people bought their own TV sets instead of watching their neighbors."

Behind many pieces of obscure grammar lies a motive. We are not speaking of the intent to deceive or the desire to sell a product, as when a building contractor puts up a sign in two-foot letters that proclaims THE MODERN MODULE CONCEPT IN HOUSING! Rather the motive is to say something in hiding, as it were. One communicates as if from behind a chair, to another chair across the way in which no one sits. Neither writer nor reader is present, only a message—itself beyond language—hanging in space between the two chairs: *The phase of the performance review procedure related to district standards constitutes performance evaluation.* No writer and no reader. Put them both firmly into the message, and the sentence might read: *Here, in this part of the review, we are evaluating your performance. You are expected to meet the standards of the district, as they are outlined in. . . .*

The distortions of American English are reinforced—even created by—the strange desire of Americans for rhetorical anonymity. Teachers beat the human voice out of their students' prose until what comes out of their charges sounds like a machine. When we started the first page of our college textbook with an anecdote that had us and the student talking together in a friendly fashion, the mail from teachers sizzled with denunciation, the most damning of which was, "You authors are condescending in your tone; you can't talk to students like that! We are teaching them *formal* writing; and you are setting a bad example by writing informally." Clearly, the advice we offer the student and reader may not be, *Try this or that, and you may write better*. It has to be translated into *This or that type of attempt may lead to an improvement of the skills of writing*.

So the infection of Unspeech reaches everywhere, from the White House to the big red schoolhouse. No one, from baseball umpire to bishop, is free of it.

Watching television, we heard a slum priest in Chicago refer to the lack of *upward mobility* of his people. Perhaps the speaker shared a weakness of his countrymen, who "rejoice," as Evelyn Waugh wrote, in euphemisms. By Americans, said Waugh, "the blind and maimed are called 'handicapped,' the destitute, 'underprivileged'. . . . the American vocabulary is pulverized between two stones, refinement and overstatement. 'O let me not be mentally ill, not mentally ill, sweet heaven' sounds odd, but in the U.S.A., 'mad' merely means 'cross.' "[20]

A major evil of Unspeech is that its decorations and accompaniments can end by displacing reality itself. An example of this can be found in an experiment reported in *The Journal of Medical Education* for July 1973. According to their account, three researchers "selected a professional actor who looked distinguished and sounded authoritative; provided him with a sufficiently ambiguous title, Dr. Myron L. Fox, an authority on the application of mathematics to human behavior; dressed him up with a fictitious but impressive curriculum vitae, and presented him [as a lecturer] to a group of highly trained educators"—specifically, fifty-five psychiatrists, psychologists, social workers, educators, and administrators. One of the researchers "coached the lecturer to present his topic and conduct his question and answer period with an excessive use of double talk, neologisms, non sequiturs, and contradictory statements. All this was . . . interspersed with parenthetical humor and meaningless references to unrelated topics." The members of the highly educated group were fooled by the fake lecturer. Said the researchers laconically, "Considering the educational sophistication of the subjects, it is striking that none of them detected the lecture for what it was."[21]

It is tempting to treat the antics of Dr. Myron Fox and his dim-witted audience as a comedy of contemporary intellectual manners. But Dr. Fox is hardly unique; some of the most important policy-makers in Washington communicate by accident as incompetently as he did on purpose. The final question concerning American English may indeed be one involving simple competence. Our most serious worry in the years to come should not be whether we can produce great novelists and poets but whether we can think and speak well enough to survive. If many educated people are so incompetent linguistically that trained specialists can be fooled by an actor spouting deliberate nonsense in a field touching theirs, we are in for a bad time.

2☆
On (Sometimes) Teaching Students to Write

So much for the situation of American English. Among the causes contributing to that situation we have held back a major one—the public school. The school is the only institution formally designed for instruction in the language. How is it doing its job?

Most of what Americans know about English teaching in the school is spotty and far from exact. Impressions come from insufficiently researched articles in national magazines; brief and usually inaccurate newspaper pieces done by reporters who know next to nothing about how English-teaching is actually performed; six-minute squibs on television news; gossip from a few PTA meetings. Although we had taught English for many years (sixth grade through graduate school), our firsthand knowledge of the contemporary public school was insufficient to draw satisfactory conclusions.

This insufficiency we were determined to remedy. So in the fall of 1976, we took official leave from the University of Illinois and piled into our aging Pontiac, which we filled with necessities like a fire extinguisher, a butane cooker, and dozens of cans of stew. The university paid our salaries, but we paid all travel expenses, eating in the car and in roadside parks. For the various foundations and other institutions to which we applied for financial assistance had declined to support a project so lacking in glamour—to do simple research by observation, to go and look at public high schools and their English programs.

Five months later, we had driven eighteen thousand miles, covering the major geographical areas, and had visited fifty high schools. The term *sample* in this chapter and the next refers to those fifty schools. We did not have the time to visit grade schools or junior highs, so they are not included in our sample. The schools in our sample ranged in size from six hundred and ninety to sixty-one hundred students and in minority population from zero to 60 percent. Since we wanted to ascertain any likely connections between English teaching and college-entrance scores, we visited no slum schools, which send relatively few students to college. As part of our agreement with the schools, we do not identify them by name but by geographical area. This accords with the practice of the National Assessment program.

To the general public, most high schools—excluding, of course, those in the slums—present a bland and accommodating face. Unless one is on the inside, one never suspects that they stumble from crisis to crisis and that even the best teachers again and again find it difficult to concentrate on educational matters. The account of school problems in this chapter and the next is accurate in its details so far as we could ascertain them. We took notes on the spot. On many occasions we conducted separate interviews of school people and later collated our information. We brought home thousands of pages of mimeographed or printed matter supplied by the schools. We also rely on experience and reading whenever corroboration is needed.

Whether any of our descriptions will fit the high school you support with your taxes is hard to say. Your school may be better or worse than any we visited or have taught in. There is, in addition, the fact of variable procedure and pedagogy within every school. A poor English department may have two excellent teachers; an excellent department, one or two weak ones. Since most American teachers go their own way unsupervised in the castle of their classroom, two sections of a course called College Writing, when taught by two teachers, may be as different as night and day—and cannot even be judged by the same criteria. The very idea of an educational or professional standard has become as foreign to teachers as the idea of freedom is to those who have lived under a totalitarian government all their lives. Teachers have lived so long with instability and change that they consider their chaotic existence to be normal. Like characters out of *1984,* they seem puzzled if one questions the disorder of things. More than once, one of us asked a teacher, "But why do you put up with this?" A blank look was the only answer.

Teachers, we might add, are not the villains of this account. That, as a group, they have not taught the language well is evident enough. But that they have persisted in trying to teach it at all—under, at times, extremely unpleasant conditions—is evidence of their patience and goodwill. Most of their sharpest critics have never been in their shoes and could not endure for two weeks what not a few of them have endured for twenty years. It is not surprising that students read and write badly; it is remarkable, all things considered, that they read and write as well as they do; and for this rather tarnished gift of culture they can thank thousands of teachers who have been doing a job that no one else has been clamoring to perform.

We offer this sincere tribute now because we will shortly be pointing out, with tiresome specificity, the plain deficiencies of programs and instruction in English across the country. We will not use space to stop at every paragraph to make a qualification that might run like this: "Yet this school does well at such-and-such activities; the principal seems an honest, hard-working man; and two of the English teachers are among the best we have seen. If two others could be fired, and the incompetent curriculum supervisor removed, the teaching of writing would (other things being equal) probably be improved—all this assuming that the surrounding community gave any encouragement to the teaching and learning of 'the language arts.' " (This last phrase is the fad term for composition, literature, and speech.)

The young American is taught writing—at least, some writing, however little—at all levels of the school system. Of these the high school is unusually important. At the high school age, roughly from fourteen through eighteen, the student is mature enough to understand how and why linguistic choices are made by competent writers. With sufficient instruction, most students can improve their use of English. To accomplish this, they require training in grammar, usage, word choice, sentence structure, as well as the devices of composition, such as learning how to focus on a topic or write a satisfactory paragraph.

Of necessity, techniques of teaching writing take second place to certain realities—for instance, how motivated and intelligent one's students are or how well they have been trained before they come into one's class. Here arises the matter of *articulation*, which means the "fit" between school units or levels with regard to curriculum and pedagogy. (For an explanation of other terms used in this chapter and the next, see page 36). While educators are concerned with articulation between grade levels, they worry rather more about articulation between the larger units—kindergarten, grade school, junior high, high school, and college.

Take, for example, a well-trained teacher, Kitty Smith, in a three-year high school of twenty-five hundred students into which "feed" three junior high schools located in different areas of the community. She faces her first sophomore class in the fall. What do the students know about grammar and composition? Where can she start her work? We shall make up her class from a number of real examples.

Kitty Smith may find in her group of thirty students two

who read quite poorly, five who are slow or unmotivated readers, fifteen who are average, and eight distinctly above average. What formal training in grammar have they had? Twelve appear to have had none; five know some traditional grammar; eight know only the transformational type (a "new" grammar that we shall discuss later on); and five cannot be classified. Of course, these descriptions are not quite accurate, partly because there is so much difference between what a student will say he knows about grammar and what grammatical operations he can perform. It turns out that twelve students in her class were actually taught transformational grammar in junior high; but since this grammar assumes a knowledge of some operations and terms of traditional grammar, students' remarks about their training can be unintentionally misleading.

When Kitty Smith considers their backgrounds in composition, the situation is even less clear. She asks, "How many of you have written themes?" Five students ask, "What is a theme?" Eight apparently have never written one, but most of the class have written paragraphs. Can they all write comprehensible and more or less grammatical sentences? No. But among the sixteen who can write good sentences fairly consistently, little correlation can be found between their past training in grammar and their ability to write.

Kitty Smith cannot assume that a majority of her students know about the common grammatical operations or can practice them. Nor can she assume that they are able to write sentences or coherent paragraphs. Full-fledged themes will be beyond most of them. Yet if she starts with the grammatical "fundamentals," she will waste the time of the best students in the class, and she does not want to lose their attention or interest at the beginning of the school year. Accordingly, since she is an able teacher with considerable common sense, she responds to the reality of the situation

Table of Definitions

Nongraded school: Any student can take any course, regardless of grade level, in his school. High schools have either three or four grades.

Elective: A course that can be chosen by the student, as opposed to a *required* course, which the student must take.

Phase: Level of difficulty of a course. Replaces the term *track*. *Tracking* meant that the school authorities put a student in the course level they thought he belonged in. *Phasing* (as used in *phase elective*) means that the student chooses his own course and its level of difficulty "according to his needs and interests." Phased courses most often have five phases, each designed to satisfy a range of students, from those who have trouble reading (numbered 1) to those who can read Shakespeare (numbered 5). When a course appears in the school catalog, it will have one or more phase numbers after it; for example, Literature of the West (1–2); Shakespeare (5); Composition for College (4–5).

Heterogeneous grouping: The method of placing students of varying abilities into one class—that is, into one period of a course meeting at a particular time.

Modular scheduling: A method of varying class lengths (or *modules*) from 15, 20, or 30 to 45 minutes (other lengths are possible). Classes can meet for one or more modules in a flexible schedule. In a week's time one might study, say, grammar for a total of 90 minutes or 300 minutes, depending on the number of modules assigned to the subject.

"The Bad Period": A phrase often used by teachers and administrators. A period (from 1967–68 to 1971–72 in most schools) of great experimentation, particularly with courses, new programs of study, and the phase-elective system. Coincided with the rise of student power and "student rights." A synonym also in use is *chaos*.

by beginning with the students' own work rather than with drills in grammar and composition. That compromise is one of the primary reasons why the classroom use of textbooks has declined in favor of using student papers and mimeographed handouts. It solves at least part of the problem that teachers face.

Articulation continues to be a thorny issue in American schools. When we asked fifty chairmen of English departments about the amount of articulation in English programs between junior and senior high schools in their system, we received these answers: twenty-five said "no articulation" or "very little"; ten said "a great deal"; eleven said "a moderate amount"; and four were uncertain.

With the move away from the new grammar, high school teachers can now be somewhat more certain that their incoming students were at least taught the same grammatical system that is employed in the high school. But they can be less certain about the standards of performance in the lower school. Very few schools apply (at any level) consistent standards in grading student papers. Since students in large groups tend to do only as much work as required, a lack of standards means that even if curricular articulation is excellent, the teacher may have to deal every year with a range of student proficiency such as Kitty Smith had to face.

If the teacher is like dozens of others whom we have known over the years, she will teach as best she can and will leave her sophomores better than she found them. But to survive in the system, she will fail no student in the course,* and the eleventh-grade teacher will have to struggle with roughly the same range of literacy (if not the same kind) that Kitty Smith had to.

At this point, a look at specific schools is in order. To see how they integrate the teaching of composition into their

---

*See below for the present state of grade inflation, pp. 64–65.

English programs, let us briefly compare four schools, two successful and two not.

School A is a community or cooperative high school, serving fifteen thousand people, in a New England town of nine thousand. The high school has a student population of about fourteen hundred. Its English program is divided into two large parts—freshmen and sophomores; and juniors and seniors. Each student must take four years of English. In the first two years, during which particular courses are required, he studies grammar, composition, usage, and literature. Both of these years are taught at six different levels or phases, the first three phases taking average to honors students, the second three taking the rest, including those who are discipline problems. The next-to-last level is for students who are behind two or three grades in reading ability.

Juniors and seniors are taught in a nongraded, phase-elective program, whose five phases are carefully controlled by the English teachers. They may refuse to allow a student to sign up for an elective that he is not fitted for, or that is obviously too easy for him. In his last two years, each student must take at least one semester of composition and one of American literature. Homework is required for all courses, and an ability to write is, as a matter of written school policy, "a graduation requirement for all students."

In the phase-elective program, School A has thirty-one courses, ranging from Shakespeare (high phase) to Sports Literature (low phase). Nineteen of these courses are offered only in alternate years. In composition, the courses are phased in three levels of difficulty. Expository Writing is top phase; Basic Composition is for the low-ability students in low phases 1 and 2. (In sharp contrast to the practice of many schools, which use Creative Writing as the dumping ground for the poor or unteachable students, School A puts Creative Writing in the top phase and demands good work from the students in it.)

School A takes a firm attitude toward the rigors of composition. Says its curriculum guide, "Writing is a skill which is developed by hard work. It is an intellectual and emotional experience which is not always pleasant or enjoyable." The guide goes on to remark that "revision and criticism" are necessary "to improve the form of the piece and the message being communicated." The English department uses a grammar text at every level. Compositions are assigned and graded in literature courses, and the school has its own competency test in English. The elective system was tightened up several years ago to prevent students from picking their way around the harder courses. The required course in composition for juniors and seniors is a recent addition.

Everything we saw in School A pointed to its being one of the half-dozen best schools in our sample. What made it outstanding? Not, one would guess, unusual pressure from the community, which appears to be no different from many others of its size and relative prosperity. The state, we were told, is "behind" many others in its support of schools; local taxes have to bear the burden.

We found a possible answer in two things: the excellence of the school administrators, and the determination of the present English teachers to do a good job. Over a two-year period, six of the twelve teachers in the English department resigned, including one tenured teacher and the department chairman. The result was the hiring of new staff members who were both better teachers and more willing to view the English department as a unit rather than as a collection of individuals. Some of the more radical ideas of the sixties, such as the open school, are being abandoned. "The open school doesn't work for anyone," said the principal. "Town, parents, students—they all suffer."

The administration of School A delegates considerable authority to the chairman of the English department, and relies on him to control the quality of the teaching. The

39

chairman, who has strong authority in the hiring, supervision, and evaluation of teachers, has four periods of released time a day for his work as chairman. Consequently, he is often able to pop into classrooms to see what is going on.

Teachers have four preparations for a total of five classes a day (one hundred to one hundred and twenty-five students). Each teaches two sections on the same level of either freshman or sophomore English, at least one high-phase and one low-phase course, and one composition course. Thus, he meets at least three grade levels in his work. In this way, each teacher has a stake in the English curriculum as a whole, including the composition courses, and the work of the department gets spread around fairly. We were impressed by the energy and morale of the teachers, who appeared to be effectively teaching the writing skills in every course, not just in composition. "I believe in an organized, teacher-directed class," said one experienced man. The student papers we read were among the best corrected we encountered anywhere. All this, for an average teachers' salary of $11,500 a year.

About one hundred miles away from School A, in another New England state, is School B, a large nongraded comprehensive high school in a city of a hundred thousand. The school, which has slightly more than six thousand students and fifty English teachers, is located in a community described as "middle and lower-middle class." School B has a handsome modern plant in fine condition; the students (including a black minority of 10 percent) appear neat and well behaved; we heard no complaints about student conduct or attitudes.

Students are tracked into six phases, ranging from Advanced Placement to Occupational. Class scheduling is modular, and the average instructor teaches classes fifty-one minutes long. Of the sixty courses listed in the English department, two are required—ninth-grade English and one speech course in the tenth grade.

In the recent past, School B has had trouble with its English curriculum, which it admits has been disorganized and ineffective. Electives are too numerous; courses are often without set texts; many students can avoid the elective courses in composition; there is no required unit or course in grammar and composition and no standard textbook for the teaching of writing. The conclusion of the department itself is that the teaching of literature has superseded instruction in the skills of writing. It is not surprising to learn that the school system as a whole lacks stability; three superintendents with differing philosophies have been appointed in five years. From 1970 to 1975, School B's English department has had four different chairmen.

When we visited School B, the English department, under a new chairman who teaches only one class, was trying vigorously to reorganize its curriculum, particularly the courses in writing. The tenth-grade program will no longer consist of electives, and one semester of writing will be required in both the eleventh and twelfth grades.

Across the country from these two schools, on the West Coast, we visited School C, one of the smallest in our sample. It has eight hundred students, of whom 35 percent are Mexican-American and 3 percent Oriental. Clean and fairly glowing with prosperity, the small agricultural town in which the school is located looks like one of Andy Hardy's memories. But School C is in educational trouble, at least as far as its English department is concerned.

The town and the school board do not properly support the teaching of English. Since the junior high has no reading program, the high school (grades 9–12) has to bear the brunt of teaching reading, and one hundred and eighty ninth-graders are in the reading program. Sixty percent of the ninth-graders read below the sixth-grade level. According to the chairman of the English department, so much effort is spent on the weak students that the average and superior students are neglected.

The recent history of the English curriculum in School C supports this judgment. In the late sixties and early seventies, the English department had twenty courses, among them honors English, Public Speaking, Grammar Review, English Literature, American Literature, The Novel, Mythology and Folklore. All are gone—"deleted," says the official explanation offered by the school. The courses disappeared, say the teachers, partly because of too little money, partly because of lack of student interest. Now four courses are left—"English" for grades nine, ten, and eleven, and an odd "independent reading" course for the twelfth grade. Class size is growing from an average of twenty-four in recent years to the present number of thirty-one. And this is one of the few high schools we know of that has a six-class load* for English teachers, who here earn an average of $13,000 a year. Although the English chairman had one free period (for chairing) three years ago, he now has none.

Conclusion: School C has some good teachers and a dying program in English. When the observer looks at the data on the school's financial support of programs, he is struck by one comparison: excluding classroom salaries, the local school board spends roughly fifty-five times as much on competitive sports and physical education as it does on English.

School D, about one hundred and fifty miles from School C, is situated in a suburb of a city of over half a million. It is a three-year high school serving eighteen hundred students, of whom 11 percent are Mexican-American and 3 percent are Oriental and black. The neighborhood is mainly middle class.

---

* The teaching load for most high school teachers is five classes a day, with one free period for preparation and paper grading. If a school district considers the duties of a department chairman important, he may have two or more free periods.

Until 1968 School D had a classic program in English—three tracked years for every student. Then it adopted electives for the eleventh and twelfth grades. Four years later, the English department began tightening this new elective system. Firm requirements were imposed for the tenth grade: a course in reading for students who did not read at grade level, and one in speech for the rest. The speech course emphasizes logic, research, and the organization of ideas. By the time we visited School D, the department had reduced the number of electives from thirty-four to eleven and set up strict requirements for the tenth and eleventh grades.

In the tenth grade, each student takes a semester of literature and composition, with intensive drill in mechanics and vocabulary. In that year grammar and usage are stressed, but they continue to be taught for at least six weeks in the eleventh grade. In the second semester, tenth graders take courses in speech and reading that are tracked according to the student's reading ability. Each eleventh-grader must take American literature in one term and a composition course in the other. In the fall term, each eleventh-grader writes what is called a hurdle essay, which determines proficiency in writing. If he passes it with a B he is allowed to take one of the twelfth-grade electives in English in the spring, but he must also take the required eleventh-grade English course of the spring term.

In effect, School D has instituted requirements for two of its three years of English, reserving the elective system mainly for the twelfth grade. The skills of reading, writing, speaking, and thinking are taught early in the students' first year at the school and are later emphasized in every course, including the electives.

If, before investigating them, you were to stroll through the last two schools described here, you might guess that both have decent English programs. Both are set in pleasant surroundings; both are, in the broad view, reasonably well supported financially. Teaching salaries are comparable. School C has a higher percentage of minority students, but according to the teachers, they have no "minority problems" worth mentioning. The school is a clean, bright-looking place. School D, with well over twice the number of students, is beginning to look run down; and its appearance is not enhanced by the steel-mesh doors and walls that were erected to keep vandals out—walk-on vandals, not students in the school. Yet it is School C, with its shiny private-school atmosphere, that is doing the poorer job. Its teaching of the language seemed desultory, unsure, vague.

In sharp contrast, School D has a well-developed curriculum and a strong English chairman who has two classes off for administration and considerable authority in hiring, supervising teachers, and determining curriculum. The principal, who believes in the English basics, gives the chairman the necessary encouragement and backing. The teachers appear happy and hard-working. Fifteen years ago, the school board limited English-class size to twenty-five, so that with a five-class schedule teachers are seeing seventy-five fewer students a day than the teachers in School C. The correcting and grading of papers is much better than average. This school is one of the few in our sample where teachers were not grading too high.

The recent history of the composition course in our sample generally parallels that of grammar and literature courses. The development has been from the traditional to the experimental, or "free learning," and then back (part way) to the traditional. One school located in the far Midwest reported its history as follows: In 1965, composition courses were of the old, standard variety. The twelfth-grade composition course used a traditional text, teaching paragraph development and the classic forms of discourse (exposition, narration, argument, description). The subject matter was largely nonliterary, although literature was occasionally used as a springboard for writing.

Toward the middle of the Bad Period, English teachers in this school, influenced as they were by the elective system and the attack on composition teaching as stultifying, dismantled the old courses and went in for "do your own thing" courses in which little writing was taught. In the early seventies, the school gave up the fad and went back to composition courses, although these are now entirely elective except for the first high school year. The older twelfth-grade composition course, however, was not reinstituted, composition being made a part of twelfth-grade literature.

This history is characteristic of the times. In the older high school composition courses, students learned the forms and wrote partly about themselves and partly about literature. Usually, each student had his own composition text, from which he studied directly and with which the teacher corrected papers. In the course as it is now taught, the "text" the student carries around is often a book of stories, poems, or plays; he may have no composition book. Books on composition are stacked in the back of the room to be used for reference. At the same time, the range of texts is wider. A student may have available to him W. Strunk, Jr., and E. B. White's famous little *Elements of Style* or John E. Warriner's huge *English Grammar and Composition*, about which we will have something to say later.

As one would expect, the phase-elective system has had profound effects on the composition course. One is that, in most schools, fewer students take the course we ordinarily called Composition. In a school located in a wealthy suburb, 80 percent of the twelfth-graders took "Comp. II" before electives were installed. Afterward, about 20 percent of them took the course. But these figures do not tell the whole story, for more than 20 percent have been taking one or another course that "deals with writing."

Just how it is being dealt with is anybody's guess, for mysterious things are done with phase-elective composition. One school of medium size has five courses in composition, all differentiated by phase level and none required. Seventy-five percent of all the students enrolled in the high school take at least one of these, the most popular of which are Personal Writing (the student writes whatever he wants) and Creative Writing. In one good school in the South, Creative Writing is phased 1 through 5—heterogeneous grouping with a vengeance. In a New England school students are required to choose in their last two years a one-semester course in each of the categories of composition, language, and literature. Their choices in the composition category are five: Advanced Composition, Creative Writing, Journalism, Research Paper, or Practical Writing. A title like the last is ordinarily a euphemism for *remedial writing*. Names are important: in one school students avoided Expository Writing until its name was changed to Pre-College Writing.

The phase-elective system has rather effectively driven out the section of the old composition course that used to teach reasoning, avoidance of fallacy, and argument or persuasion. In most of the English departments we visited, this section is now placed in a high-phase speech or debate course, which is taken by a relatively small number of students.

As was the case with the study of grammar, neither teachers nor administrators know how much writing most students are doing. The customary remark is, "The quantity of writing varies; it depends on the teacher." It is unusual for a department to publish requirements outlining the number or type of themes to be written in particular courses. Unusual also are any established requirements for the quality of work or type of grading. Some teachers use the "folder system," in which the papers that students write are kept for reference and consultation with the teacher. Sometimes the teacher marks them heavily. Sometimes, she neither marks nor grades the paper but goes over them with students individually.

The variation in what is expected from students in their writing is very great, both from teacher to teacher and school to school. A creative-writing teacher may tell you that "any insistence on correctness kills good writing," while another teacher in the same school marks every mistake she finds. One English department publishes its requirements as to type and quality of student writing, while another ignores the whole matter. In northern New England, we found an excellent school that requires a genuine composition course in each grade. Although the school has a phase-elective system, the English teachers themselves place each student in the course judged best for him: "No good student is allowed in one of the lower courses just because it is easy. We *demand* that the student do the best work of which he is capable."

Good schools are much like each other, as are good teachers. The best composition programs tend to be similar, whether they are two hundred or two thousand miles apart. In a good program, one finds that the department—backed by the administration—has high expectations. It assumes that the student can, and will, learn to write better than he has been writing. Such departments may publish a mimeographed statement about the type and quality of work that they expect from students in each grade, and the statement will be given to both students and parents. Seldom is any concession made to problems of dialect or minority origin. Said one teacher, "We pay no attention to the 'students' right to their own language'; we require standard English at all times" (see Chapter Four). Nor is there much reaction to the "problem" of college-entrance scores. "I don't give a damn about the scores," said one successful chairman. "What I care about is—can the student *write?*" In this chairman's department, all the teachers mark and grade most of the compositions that are assigned. "If a kid spends time writing a paper," said one, "it is my job to spend at least thirty minutes reading and grading it."

Another characteristic of the better composition programs is that teachers carefully prepare their students for writing. Many English teachers apparently have never learned the fundamental principle that you don't assign a composition by saying, "Write a paper for next Tuesday on such-and-such a topic." What one gets from an ill-considered assignment is ill-considered writing. In most cases, preparing for a composition means discussing possible theses, methods of organization, and types of evidence to support generalizations. Models of sample paragraphs and outlines may prove useful. Successful teachers may carry a student through his planning over a period of days, checking the composition as it develops and, after it is written, carrying him again through a rewritten version. Good teaching of composition is rather like good editing: from the conception of the paper to the revised draft, the teacher works with the student, as a friendly advisor, pointing out weaknesses and praising strengths.

It is significant that when asked about their high school training, college students seldom report this kind of teaching in their high school composition classes. And we did not see much of it being done in the schools. Consider these extracts from two typical themes by college-bound students aged about seventeen and attending schools a thousand miles apart:

(1) The present and potential industrial capabilities of the area are being attacked by a closed-minded minority who refuse to acknowledge the fact that industry is a vital and a very essential factor in this country's progress. In their hurried and emotional assault, this minority has seen fit to ignore the

opposing views entirely, and continue to proceed in a blind fashion. The feeling that the only good environment is one of pure natural status is not practical, and cannot prevail over the inevitable progressive movement of industry.

(2) There are some factors worth considering before choosing a college. First of all, some basic facts such as the size and location of the college must fulfill the student's needs. He must fit into the college's atmosphere and the college cannot be either too close or too far away to cause any problems in transportation. Also, the student must know if he wants to attend a coed college or not, and a university, or a private college. Another factor worth considering before choosing a college is the financial aspect. The college's tuition must be affordable by the student. If he needs financial aid, the student should look for certain colleges that offer loans. The most important factor of all is the college's curriculum. The student must find a college that specifies in his intended major so he will get a good education. The college's curriculum should also offer many social activities for the student to get involved. These major factors are very important for every student to consider before choosing a college.

In neither passage is there a hint that teachers have prepared the student for a proper job of communication. Neither student has the faintest idea of his audience, though one of the first questions any writer must come to grips with is, For whom am I writing this? Neither has been trained to work from the general to the particular or inversely; each paragraph is a series of unsupported generalities. And each student is grossly careless with words, "flatting and sharping," as Mark Twain put it in his great essay on James Fenimore Cooper, without hitting the right note.

To particularize by way of showing what a teacher ought to mark and discuss: How, in example 1, can a *capability* be *attacked* by a *minority?* Why need a *factor* be both *vital* and *essential?* How can an *environment* be something of *pure natural status;* a *feeling prevail* over a *progressive movement?* In example 2, what can be meant by *facts* that *fulfill needs; fit into the college's atmosphere; factor is aspect;* and *college that specifies in his intended major?*

What happens in the production of such compositions is clear enough. Teacher and student arrive at a tacit agreement about the role of writing: it is not important. Slop something on the page, and hand the paper in; teacher will hand it back with a grade on it. Transaction closed. From beginning to end, nothing occurs to disturb the even tenor of the educational ways; words are sent from one person to another without disturbing the mind of either.

To the teacher's credit it must be said that she tried to make the writer of example 2 understand some of the problems of word choice and generality, but she gave the paper a C—which is two grades too high. Both writers are reasonably literate (they can spell and form grammatical sentences) and are therefore capable of being taught to write clear, careful publishable prose—*publishable* meaning that it communicates ideas efficiently and attractively. Over the years, we have seen thousands of student papers that achieved this modest competence after the students were properly instructed.

But there is the problem. Instructing students properly in the arts of composition is difficult and becoming more so. For every teacher in high school who does a satisfactory job of teaching English, there are half a dozen who do not. A note that we made after we had looked at a few sample papers from a composition class in a Southwestern school reads, "Teacher keeps talking about giving 'the kids what they want in an English class.' What they want, of course, is not what they should get."

Ineffective teaching is unmistakably connected with the practice brought over from the Bad Period of avoiding textbooks and printed models. Said a teacher in the South, "We don't believe in using written models for student writing, the kind you find in high school writing textbooks. Such models are too good and too hard for students. For models, we use their own mimeographed papers." Using such logic, a man beginning his surgical training would never watch an experienced surgeon at work for fear he might learn expert technique: instead he would painfully and bloodily muck along, trying one procedure after another until finally he "teaches" himself surgery, killing a few dozen patients in the process. It took centuries to arrive at the modern textbook but only a decade to abandon it to mimeograph paper enshrining the work of adolescents. Of course, student models can be helpful pedagogical aids, particularly when they show students how an assignment has been handled well by their peers or when they exemplify certain rhetorical or grammatical faults. But student papers—almost by definition—should not be the only models students follow.

Composition, it must be said again, involves the mastery of particular skills, from organizing material to handling certain grammatical operations properly. We can get an idea of how teachers encourage—or discourage—the mastery of such skills by their handling of two important ones, grammar and usage.

The traditional school grammar is based on a method of linguistic analysis that goes back to the ancients. Familiar terms like *noun*, *verb*, and *clause* have their origins in Latin. Though parsing sentences has not been done in this country for decades, a school grammar may still ask students to identify the parts of speech or explain how clauses work in a sentence. In recent years the major school texts have supplied much more than instruction in the fundamentals of grammar. If you look at the table of contents of the most popular school grammar in the United States, you will find lessons and information on speaking and listening, libraries and reference works, paragraphs and themes, letter writing, research papers, punctuation, dialects, and logic. There is also a long section on usage. This large book (over seven hundred pages), called *English Grammar and Composition*, was first published in 1958 and by 1977 was in its sixth edition. Its senior author is John E. Warriner, and the book has become known throughout the country simply as *Warriner*. *Warriner* has a version for every grade from the seventh through the twelfth; the one we have been discussing is used in the eleventh grade.

In the sixties there were two important changes made in the way teachers taught grammar. The first change occurred when the high schools, following the example of many universities in their teacher-education programs, began to water down their requirements in grammar. Earlier, most high schools had taught directly out of a textbook like *Warriner*. At the beginning of the school year students would review the basics of grammar in the text, do exercises in workbooks, and practice sentence patterns in short papers.

The new grammarians, believing that such procedures were boring and worthless, launched a campaign against traditional teaching (see Chapter Four). They were so successful in their campaign that anyone still teaching traditional grammar in the middle of the Bad Period might suffer considerable harassment from both students and fellow teachers. One teacher told us that she was openly ridiculed by other teachers for teaching "mossback grammar." In consequence, many teachers stopped doing grammar entirely, filling the gap with literary materials. This was not hard to do, since the newly popular elective courses seldom did much with grammar. A similar shift in emphasis also occurred in many junior high schools.

A second change occurred in the use of grammar texts. The best-known of the new linguistic theories involved "transformational grammar," which was poured into several new textbooks, the most successful being those written by Paul Roberts. Roberts' English Series—referred to in the profession as *Roberts*—was widely adopted in grade schools and junior high schools; and some high schools used two of his books not in the series, *English Sentences* and *English Syntax*. When the battle of the books was joined, the two sides were referred to as Roberts people and Warriner people.

Under the influence of the new grammar and the new elective programs, and pressured by radicals from within and without the educational system, many English teachers felt that they could no longer teach grammar from the traditional textbook. In some instances, the choice was taken away from them. Several states have textbook-adoption lists. The "state list," as it is called, publishes the names of those texts that a school is "encouraged" to adopt. In Florida, for example, a school may prefer to adopt a state-list text because the state supplies the books on the list, thus saving considerable expense for the local system. In several states, the new grammarians, active in state educational politics, succeeded in removing traditional grammars from the list, thus leaving teachers no choice but to pick one of the new grammars. At the time of our visit to the state, Florida still did not have a *Warriner*-type book on its approved list.

In a few cases, the attack on the traditional grammar text went pretty far. In 1971, an administrator from the central office in a midwestern school ordered the destruction of every *Warriner* in the high school. "Then," said a teacher, "we had no grammar or composition books at all and didn't get any new ones until 1974." In the same year, a large southern high school started an experimental program and asked that their copies of *Warriner* be put in storage. This was done, and shortly thereafter these books were also destroyed. "We don't know how they did it," said one teacher. "One administrator told us the books were buried, another that they were burned. Anyhow they are gone, and last year [1975], I managed to scrape up only twenty-eight other grammars for one hundred and forty students." This school is in one of the wealthiest communities in the United States.

In the late sixties, then, teachers were caught in the vortex of several forces, and they reacted in predictable ways. Most of them had had little training in the new grammar, so that when forced to teach it they tended to become bewildered and resentful. Yet it was not always possible for them to go back to traditional teaching. Sometimes the textbooks were lacking; but even if they were available, students—who had had a taste of freedom in the elective system—were not eager to return to the "boring and irrelevant" study of traditional grammar, with its insistence on drill and correctness. Sometimes, members of an English department were so confused about the conflicting claims of authority in the new grammar that they threw up their hands in despair. One junior high teacher said, "We didn't know what to teach, so we didn't teach anything."

Here is a typical sequence of events, as recounted by a high school teacher in a large southwestern high school: "The State Office of Education sent out a state textbook list with no traditional grammar on it. When we talked to them at the State Office, they said they wouldn't approve a *Warriner*-type book—we had to go to some kind of new-grammar approach. But after trying this approach, most of our teachers rebelled and quit using the new texts. We went to electives about the same time, and so ended up teaching no grammar directly, and a lot of literature. What little grammar we did was indirectly taught when we graded student papers." The chairman of a department in a southern school told us that in the Bad Period "a student could graduate from high school without ever using any kind of grammar book or having any instruction in grammar. All he had to do was to pick the 'right' courses in the chaotic elective program."

At the beginning of the seventies, many schools shifted away from the new grammar. "The main problem with it," remarked a teacher, "was that it did not apply to anything. Transformational grammar has nothing to do with *writing*." A good school in New England tried *Roberts* for a year in 1969 and then dropped it abruptly, shifting to *Warriner* in 1970 for all grades. Books are expensive, and it is rare to discard a new book after only a year of use.

The situation as regards grammar texts is better now, but some confusion remains. Many schools have started buying better books or taking older ones out of storage, the move coinciding with the effort to tighten the elective system. We found only one high school that still taught a new grammar. The teachers disliked it but seemed too apathetic to press for change. "Really," said one of them, "we don't teach enough grammar here to matter one way or the other."

All the same, the habit of going without texts has changed the attitudes of some English teachers toward grammar books. "We don't teach a book any more," is a common remark. Typically, students and teachers merely "resort" to a book, which is to be found on a shelf in the back of the room. Said a department chairman in a southern school, "In our basic composition course, there is no book, and I don't want a book. In fact, we in this school would prefer to teach many courses—particularly grammar—without a book." In a large southwestern city an administrator said: "Nowhere in this system will you find a standard grammar-composition text being used—there hasn't been one since 1970." In our sample of fifty schools, only fourteen used a grammar-composition series. Eight other schools said that they plan to return to a traditional textbook or series.

Why did some teachers abandon the grammar text? One reason was subtly practical: if you haven't a book, you don't have to teach the subject. Another was that students hated the grammar text as a symbol of organized learning. "We used to assign a grammar to each student, but we gave this up; they would not carry them to class." Another, and very common, reason: not enough books. If you have thirty-five students in a class and twelve grammars on the shelves in the back of the room, you don't teach from the book. The most powerful reason—other than the sheer lack of sufficient texts—is that, in current educational cant, "textbooks are not *in*." At the end of 1976, the Associated Press reported that Mrs. Myrra Lee had been named Teacher of the Year (social science) in California. Mrs. Lee, a teacher of twenty years' experience, declared, "I wouldn't even know how to use a textbook at this point. Textbooks are a thing of the past, or should be."[1] Abetting the avant-garde point of view, the mimeograph, ditto, and photocopying machines have altered the nature of American teaching. Like Mrs. Lee, who uses "duplicated" materials, English teachers rain down dittoed sheets, mimeographed lessons, and photocopied matter on their students. However chaotically the job is performed, such teachers are in effect compiling their own texts.

Even so, teachers agree that textbooks of various kinds are being used more now than they were in the Bad Period, occasionally with pleasure for teacher and student alike. When one department adopted an anthology for a class in literature, a senior student exclaimed happily, "I finally got an English book!"

With the death of the new grammar in the high schools (it is very dead there) and with the birth of the back-to-basics movement has come a revival of interest in traditional grammar. Thirty-one schools in our sample had a required unit or course in the subject. Sometimes students are responsible for the revival. One large school in a wealthy suburb registered about fifty-five students in an elective course in grammar in 1973. In 1974, two hundred students requested the course; in 1975, four hundred and twenty-eight. Bewildered teachers stated that they were in no way responsible for the phenomenon; the students, most of them college-bound and ambitious, had decided that they needed some grammar. In a smaller school two thousand miles away, Basic Grammar used to be the least popular elective, but in the fall of 1976 it was the first English elective to be filled. The other nineteen schools in our sample were teaching only a little grammar, and that somewhat desultorily. The claim of this group was that they were, "at the teacher's discretion, correlating the teaching of grammar with literature."

Correlation is one of the voodoo words in modern pedagogy. But actually, little correlation is carried out, since it takes a teacher of genius to explain the relationship of, for example, grammar to rhetoric in a literary work, just as it takes students of remarkable attentiveness to learn something from an exposition of the relationship, assuming that an explainable one exists.

Those English departments that do have a required unit or course are generally somewhat vague about pedagogical technique. Obviously, some teachers use textbooks, workbooks, and drills. But a larger number prefer to teach the subject indirectly by correcting mistakes as they appear on papers. Typical statements from teachers: "I hardly ever give a grammar exercise to a class." "We respond to the student's grammatical problem as the need arises." We heard the second remark recently in a school where teachers agreed that the most serious problems were in the use of sentence fragments and fused sentences. These are such gross errors that we wondered whether teachers were doing anything about matters like dangling modifiers and faulty pronoun references.

Looking at the work of teachers over the years, it occurs to us that they have more difficulty teaching usage than any other element of good prose. (We are employing the term *usage* in its broadest sense, to include the debatable elements of grammar, phrasing, and word choice.) Why this should present the greatest difficulty, one can only guess.

Perhaps teachers have not had much specific college instruction in the craft of handling words as words or of making choices among locutions. Certainly, their own high school textbooks give little help; even the better ones say next to nothing about, for instance, the proper use of figurative language. Most textbook writers issue no warnings; they seem to think that the matter is properly covered if figures of speech are classified into metaphor, personification, and simile.

In any case, teachers are as a rule uncertain about the use of words and tend to overlook most of the errors that students make in diction. Here are random examples of diction that went unmarked:

—Perhaps the greatest diffidence should not involve the occult but the anxiety should be towards the men who allowed the occult to ravage their common sense.

—William Bradford's writings different William Byrd's because Bradford wrote more conceited metaphors.

—Most of the story presented a see-saw atmosphere.

—Nearly all of Fitzgerald's characters verify a lack of virtue.

—Her voluptuous chest, tightly squeezed in the material, hung out on all sides.

These and the following were written by college-bound students, who habitually lust after the abstract. One writer speaks of "subsequent lurement"; and another says with satisfaction that "joyous maddness [sic] is prevalent"; while a third concludes that "for some students, the lack of money necessitates early graduation." We may add that these elementary sins against common sense and common English occurred in papers from six different states, scattered over three geographical regions.

Why are American students thousands of miles apart producing this kind of English? Because they are being trained to produce it as calculatedly as one might teach one's dog to roll over and play dead. Behind the dull abstraction and the occasional narcotic metaphor is the guiding hand of teachers who believe that the worst words in the language are those that come trippingly to the tongue. Their first linguistic commandment is, Thou shalt not commit the colloquial. No piece of writing should ever sound like human speech; if it does, ruthlessly strike it out. Their second commandment is, Thou shalt never admit to being part of what you write. It was not you who wrote this composition; rather, you caused it to be written. Therefore, never use the word *I*; for if you do, people may suspect that you had an intimate connection with the thing.

Teachers can be quite firm about this. One department has a mimeographed "English Checklist" that invites the student to answer certain questions, among them the following: Have I *avoided* using *I?* Have I *avoided* using contractions? Have I *avoided* using colloquialisms?

The result of such admonitions would strengthen the belief that American students are supremely teachable because from coast to coast they are avoiding the obscenity of the vertical pronoun and the dreadful taint of the vernacular. Occasionally, a blithe spirit deviates on paper into natural idiom: "This cost them a lot of money." *"Colloq!"* says the red marginal comment. "The early pioneers went broke," writes a student, and his teacher responds marginally, "Went *bankrupt!*" "I think," begins one unfortunate in his first draft but thinks better of it in his second: "The personal opinion of this writer is. . . ."

In revising his paper, a student changes "You become aware of" to "It becomes increasingly apparent." "Good," says the teacher. "Avoid personal comments." Objections are made by a teacher to "small commonplace words" on one paper, and she further remarks that *"created* is a more esthetic word than *invented."* One teacher's consistency found such hobgoblins everywhere; she missed two mechanical errors in the first sentence of a theme but circled every contraction in it, while ignoring expressions like "the entertainee's [as opposed to *entertainer's*] preoccupation with his own real present environment."

In a thousand classrooms, through the kind attentions of those who know not what they do, a new American style is being invented—sorry!—created. Our young people are learning to rise up at the Pavlovian bell of the polysyllable; at the proper signal they ascend with ease into a Cloud-cuckooland of the Abstract. Here is part of the first page of a term paper with footnotes and all the trappings of scholarship (spelling unchanged): "However, a characteristic mood of self-confidence, complancency and optimism was the Victorian writers greatest protest. . . . Hardy was far ahead of his fellow writers by using a dominate style of twentieth century poetry. He structured his poetry to demonstrate fate's role in the process of life's development. . . . In this Victorian's poems man emergs as the essence of the great network of cause and effect. This network envolves man's life and its outcome."

This young student was college-bound; but do not believe that the average or "terminal" student escapes. He too can write in the abstract: "Exercising certain precautions before operating the corn chopper is necessary for safe, mind-free chopping. Specifically, insuring the safety of all children in the area is of utmost concern." After one senior teacher deplored this sort of writing, we asked her why there was so much of it. "I'm not really sure," she said. "But I do know that nowhere in our education, from kindergarten to graduate school, do we Americans stress training in word choice. Some teachers just never learn how to handle problems of usage in compositions. Maybe you just have to be born to it."

At the University of Chicago, a group of researchers

headed by Professor Joseph Williams took a number of papers written by college students and rewrote them in an abstract "noun style." "It is the style," said Williams, "of the worst kind of educationalese, governmentalese, medicalese, sociologicalese. It has been called Latinate, wordy, pretentious, circumlocutory, indirect, pompous, abstract, inflated. . . ." The researchers also rewrote the same papers in a "verb style," avoiding the abstract noun whenever possible. The noun-style papers had one nounification in every five to seven words; the verb-style papers averaged one in every fifty to one hundred words. Everything else in the papers was kept the same—logic, organization, ideas, paragraphing, number of sentences, and most of the vocabulary.

Williams then asked eighty-three readers to evaluate the two versions of the student essays. Many of these readers were teaching in high school, junior college, or college. Ten of them were inexperienced graduate students in a program leading to a Master of Arts degree in teaching; thirty-six "regularly read essays as part of a state-wide regency examination program. . . ." Williams discovered that "our evaluators responded either favorably or indifferently to [the noun] style almost 70 percent of the time." As a group, the high school teachers preferred the verb-style version only about 18 percent of the time. Williams concluded, "If what has been described here holds for the teaching of English composition in general, then our profession is contributing to an implicit value system in public discourse that is contrary to much of what we assert is important to preserve: direct, open, honest writing."[2]

Indeed, by failing to attend to the proper use of words, teachers are contributing indirectly to the widespread growth of bad prose and, through it, of bad thinking. The old habit of vocabulary drill is out of fashion. Students nowadays are seldom tested on the vocabulary of "difficult" works like *David Copperfield*—supposing that they read Dickens at all.

A new "middle school" in our city is not teaching literary works but is substituting movies and film strips about the authors' lives. In a course on Robert Louis Stevenson and Mark Twain the students read nothing by either author; they studied short biographies. The writing assignment in the course was to "compare your life with Mark Twain's."

Even when it is attempted directly, one cannot always approve of the way usage is being taught. We saw an experienced teacher assigning narrative papers using certain "required words"—*milieu, avoirdupois, vignette, foyer, cuisine, façade, apéritif, table d'hôte*—not one of them a true English word. In the papers we saw, these words were usually heaved into a breach in the sentence as carelessly as you would throw a stone at a tree. If the writer hit anything it was only by accident: "I lifted my avoirdupois off the chair and asked the man at the bar for an apéritif." A good, though unconscious, satire on modern pedagogy.

As is so often true, behind bad practice lies bad theory. If the teacher does not believe in the idea of an American standard usage in English, she will not teach it. If she believes that drill is stultifying and damaging to a student's psyche, she will use no repetitive instruction in her classroom, and about one hundred and fifty students a year will pass through her hands undrilled and untrained in usage. To their great credit—and against the combined advice of their own professional organization, the National Council of Teachers of English, and of the professors who preach at them in institutes, methods courses, summer short-courses, and in-service training sessions—a growing number of teachers are returning to older, proven methods. As one teacher told us, "I am going to be a snob about English usage from now on. I don't agree with 'the student's right to his own language' any more. There are too many children in our system without even the basic skills." She added that most of the staff in her school agreed with her.

Much pedagogical theory about writing requires faith in certain ideas. Chief among these is the belief that correcting the written work of students is at best an activity to be endured by everyone concerned; if possible, one should avoid it entirely. Perhaps this is why the typical English teacher's weakest performance in the American school is ordinarily in correcting and grading papers.

To correct a paper means to explain to the student where he went wrong—and right—in these categories: thesis, or main point; organization of paper, including paragraphing; content (quality of statements and supporting facts or examples); diction, or choice of words; sentence structure and style; and mechanics (grammar, spelling, and punctuation). *Correcting* implies the use of positive remarks, where warranted, about the successful handling of one or more of these six categories. For it is obvious that students can be helped as much by knowing where they have succeeded as by knowing where they have failed, though it is likely that some are helped a little less by the approving comments, since most students tend to be aware of doing something well when they do it.

The romantic notion that negative comments should not be made on a paper is peculiarly American. Why we should be infected with such nonsense is a matter of history—the history of "educational research" since 1900. But what it amounts to is that we have suffered a cultural loss of memory about childhood, forgetting that when we were young, we needed more or less constantly the touch of correction to stay on track, whether in deportment (quaint term!) or book learning. At any rate, the teaching of writing, as one of our mentors remarked years ago, is "by its nature both positive and negative, the negative being necessary when judging the essays that students write."

When one grades a paper, one evaluates its worth. First, broadly, is it a passing or failing (*F*) performance, given the student's age and grade level? Second, if it is passing, is it poor (*D*), fair or satisfactory (*C*), good (*B*), or outstanding (*A*)? This five-point system, long standard in the United States, works somewhat better than a percentage system, for the difference between an 82 and 88 may easily prove unclear to teacher and student. Three-point grading gives too few choices, while the so-called pass-fail system works so badly that no one any longer takes it seriously.

During the Bad Period the grading of papers became so flaccid that a new phrase was coined to describe a new condition—grade inflation. In college two generations ago, we always felt lucky to get above a *C* in an English course. Arn received a *B* and a *C* in his two terms of freshman English and later worked very hard in most courses to get a *B* or better. When grades were posted, the commonest grade on the list for an English course was *C*, with no more than a sprinkling of *A*'s and *B*'s. (Another sign of our time: you cannot post grades in certain universities now; the administration is afraid of being sued for invasion of privacy.)

In 1970, looking over posted grades one afternoon when finals were over, we found several class lists with no grade below *B* and a few others with none below *A*. At that time it was useless for a professor to complain of the absurdity inherent in the belief that all examinations are equal and all linguistic performances the same. He simply went to his office and raised his own grades so that there would be students registering for his classes next term. The chain of future events may not be clear, but in recent years there have been strong implications for both high school and college teachers who graded harder than the others did: no students, no classes, no official teaching load, no job. The laws of tenure may or may not apply.

A distribution of typical high school grades over seven years (1968–69 to 1974–75) indicates how grades have become inflated in one large district.

The San Antonio [Texas] Independent School District[3]

DISTRIBUTION OF HIGH SCHOOL GRADES

% of A's and D's or below

	SAN ANTONIO		STATE (English only)		NATIONAL*	
	A	D or F	A	D or F	A	D or F
1968–69	15%	11%	12%	9%	No national report	
1969–70	17%	13%	13%	8%	20%	5%
1970–71	18%	9%	Not available		No national report	
1971–72	18%	9%	25%	4%	No national report	
1972–73	20%	8%	28%	4%	19%	7%
1973–74	26%	8%	30%	3%	29%	3%
1974–75	32%	7%	32%	3%	32%	3%

*National results were based on a 10% sample.

A comparison (from the same source) of grade inflation in English and mathematics is instructive:

English

	SAN ANTONIO		STATE		NATIONAL	
	A	D or F	A	D or F	A	D or F
1969–70	17%	13%	13%	8%	20%	5%
1974–75	32%	7%	32%	3%	32%	3%

Mathematics

	SAN ANTONIO		STATE		NATIONAL	
	A	D or F	A	D or F	A	D or F
1969–70	13%	22%	13%	16%	13%	17%
1974–75	18%	18%	23%	9%	20%	10%

Inflation is inevitable when one considers how high school English departments typically handle grading. To begin with, ordinarily there are no "procedures" at all. In a big-city school we were told by the English chairman, "We have no standardization of teaching materials or grading. Teachers are completely free to do as they wish." Characteristically, they may wish to ignore form in favor of content. When we discussed students' papers with one experienced teacher in the Rocky Mountains, she said that she did not mind much when they failed to end sentences with a period: "Content is just as important as mechanics!" We looked at an eleventh-grader's term paper in another school. Graded *A*, and without a single other teacher's mark on it, it was a classic piece of plagiarism: the style was completely professional, there were no footnotes, and the bibliography referred only to encyclopedias.

The observer of student work and its handling finds one instance after another of careless or nonexistent correcting. Here are examples from our survey: (1) An experienced teacher has a small class of honors students; their papers are marked for only about one-third of their errors. (2) An attractive young teacher with five years' experience restricts her comments to mechanics but misses many of the mechanical errors. She offers no general comments on papers or suggestions on how the writers might improve their work. She is mute when one of her students writes, "What justice would endanger the honest American to benefit the proven guilty?" (3) An English-department chairman misses nine mechanical errors on one page. When a student writes, "So-and-so lost his life by cancer," she changes it to "*with* cancer"; it is the only correction on the page. When a student writes "dark complected," she ignores the mistake. (4) A teacher gives an *A* to a ninth-grader whose paper is full of sentences such as this: "I liked this story very much such, expecially when Sterling father let him live alone in there big house."

Yet one more example may have particular force, because the school involved is reputed to be one of the finest in the nation. The community, part of a wealthy suburb near a very large city, showers money and attention on this school, which sends the great majority of its graduates to college. Here is a paragraph written by a student in an eleventh-grade honors course:

> When the business man comes home for dinner, he eats, and then watches television until bedtime. During one of the shows, the husband kisses his wife for no particular reason. Since this kiss was out ofthe routine and the trance which comes along with the routine, the kiss is special and it has a great meaning of love behind it when compared to a routine kiss. The husband was not tranced, he was awake, and being awake, gave the kiss a more alive meaning.

The teacher made two marks on the paragraph. In the first, he separated *of* and *the;* in the second, he inserted a comma after *the kiss is special.* The teacher—a middle-aged man of long experience and known as a hard grader—gave the paper a *B.*

No two of the examples shown above came from the same school or state. This fact suggests that poor work by teachers on student papers is not the monopoly of any part of the United States. Nor are examples of good correcting and grading necessarily found in particular schools and regions. In a rather grimy school with a large minority population, we found a young teacher doing excellent work in a course called Writing for College. She managed to touch on the major problems in every paper, offering comments or questions: "Does not follow from previous sentence." "Parallelism works nicely." "None of this in your outline—does not fit here." "Good use of example." "You said this on page 2; why repeat?" "Fine organization: easy to follow because of transitions." "What is the point of this section?" "But what does the author mean the fish to symbolize?" Yet for all her efforts, her students write poorly. Does this mean that her work is done in vain? No, because some of her instruction will "take," if not this year, then the next. (An excellent teacher we know demurs: "It is more likely that her work *has* been done in vain—unless her students have a teacher next year who also corrects papers well and so builds upon her work. I have found that students—especially the younger ones—need constant reinforcement and practice.") Students may not appreciate good teaching at the time, but eventually some at least will be grateful for it. Anyhow, this teacher tried, and that is the point. In the unspoken contract between instructor and pupil is this clause: I am responsible for teaching you something; you are responsible for learning it. If it is at all possible, an English teacher should leave a student better off than she found him.

We cherish the remark of one principal about a teacher of his, a firm-looking lady in her middle years. We were inspecting her themes, which were exceptionally well corrected. "Some students say she is prejudiced against them because she grades hard," said the principal. "But that isn't true. She is just prejudiced against sorriness."

So should we all be.

3.☆
Authors of Confusion: The English Program in Disorder

Now for a broader look at the problem. We know that the high schools teach writing with—at best—indifferent success. But why? Is there any reason why a determined group of teachers and administrators could not simply decide to do the job better and then do it? To supply an answer (a partial one, to be sure), we will take a look at the high school English program in relation to the school itself.

The American public school is an enigma wrapped inside a paradox cooked in a political pie. None of our institutions is more complex or more difficult to understand in any final sense. The school once had a definite shape and purpose. A city school in California was more or less like one in Illinois; a rural school in Maine was not very different from one in Kentucky. Schools in poverty-stricken areas were often not significantly different in program from schools in prosperous suburbs. If a child moved from one state to another, he could pick up the course in English literature just about where he left off. Arn can attest to these observations, having in his time attended over thirty schools, from the first to twelfth grades, in twelve states of the Union.

The school has lost its sense of unity, largely under the influence of ideological and political forces. A half-century of educational utopianism and political pressure has so warped the school that it is now barely recognizable as an educational entity. Through the courts, various indirect political devices (the school board being a political organism), and direct pressure brought by parents and "concerned citizens," Americans have propelled the school toward a multitude of goals, some of them contradictory, most of them impossible to reach in any conceivable circumstances.

The average school does not know what it is or where it is going. It knows, however, that whatever it does, someone will object, bring a lawsuit, or simply put a gun to its head. Once a center of reason and morality, it is now less reasonable and less concerned with right and wrong than the society around it. That is, society generally requires more of a sixteen-year-old outside the school—in his home, part-time job, or on the street—than it does inside. While society may require of him certain definite intellectual skills on the job—for example, the skills of a grocery stockboy—it will often harass teachers who try to hold him to intellectual standards in an English class.

The misguided attempt to train in a classroom future poets, mechanics, army privates, and medical doctors while trying at the same time to solve the sexual, racial, and political ills of our country has produced schools about which it is nearly impossible to be truthful. One truth contradicts another. We have been watching our local high school for thirteen years, have had four children in it, and cannot think of a safe generalization about it.

What are the causes of confusion in high school English teaching? To begin with, there is the presence of the phase-elective system in English departments. The phase-elective system in English came into being in the late 1960's, at the beginning of the Bad Period. In the typical school, the changeover was sudden and dramatic. One term you had the old set of courses (American Literature in the eleventh grade, English Literature in the twelfth), and the next you had anywhere from thirty to ninety electives. Only one school we visited was switching to electives in 1976, and its list of courses is typical of those we found in the catalogs of the sixties. This school's English department lists fifty-four courses, of which these are a sample, the titles being reported exactly as they were given to us: Cub Reporting, Annual Production (I and II); Greek Tragedy; Death Lit; Bible Lit; Women's Lit; Literature of Evil, Devil; Children's Lit; Alienation Lit; Values Lit; Anglo Saxon to Medieval Lit; War Lit; Science Fiction Lit; Essay Writing; Mystery Lit; Plots from Easy Shakespeare.

When they adopted phase electives, many schools also went to a shorter term, often referred to as a quarter, or minicourse, term. This could be as short as three weeks or as long as twelve. One school in the Southwest varies its term lengths throughout the year; they range from eight to ten and one-half weeks. In its eleventh and twelfth grades, a southern school has nine-week electives that include such courses as Survey of English Literature; Shakespeare; Modern Drama (Ibsen to the Present); and Mythology and Classical Literature. This might be called the Big Bite theory of education.

A small but significant number of schools have combined phase electives with modular scheduling. Such combining raises astronomically the number of variables in scheduling courses, teachers, and rooms—particularly when one remembers that schools teach courses other than English. Even if the whole business is fed into computers, it is not unusual for a school's courses to be scheduled around the English offerings.

Modular scheduling can produce interesting arrangements in the teaching of English. One department head told us of his two composition classes (seventy students altogether). During a nine-week term, he taught composition modules for a total of seventy minutes a week; the students were taking seven to nine other courses at the same time, many of them on the modular arrangement. The teacher remarked that students had trouble keeping up with this complicated schedule and dropped behind in both their reading and writing assignments. "It's a strange system," he said. "I see my students so seldom I don't recognize most of them in the hallways." He added thoughtfully, "I do a lot of teaching in the halls—you just can't cram enough into a little over an hour a week." One must add that his was not a typical school.

For most schools, the phase-elective system in its full-blown form lasted only four or five years, until the early seventies. Then it was modified in several ways. First, the number of electives was reduced, and the sillier ones dropped. Second, the schools insisted that one of the first two high school years include a required course in the basics for all students. Some three-year high schools required the first two years, allowing for electives only in the twelfth grade. Third, some English departments created area requirements so that students could not avoid taking a certain amount of composition and grammar, even into the twelfth grade. They could pick one course from among four or five in the composition group. Fourth, by revamping the advising system, schools have tended to force students into the courses they should be taking. In effect, students are told, "Here is our advice on your program; you don't have to take it." But a school can make it nearly impossible not to.

Every school we visited that had instituted an elective system eight or ten years before had tightened it up considerably. Here is how the chairman of the English department in a good school described the process:

> Before we put electives in, we studied the system for a year—but we still made mistakes. We soon discovered that

many students chose electives on the basis of whether they were easy—which meant, practically speaking, whether they had no writing in them. They went for Modern Drama, Speech, Creative Writing.

So we tightened up the system in the early seventies; dropped some courses and combined others. Now we have only nine electives [for eleventh and twelfth grades] that can be taken to fulfill English requirements; all eleventh graders must take a semester of language and composition; and the elective courses in creative writing, drama, and journalism may not be used to fulfill English requirements.

Perhaps you are wondering why unrestrained electives were so popular during the Bad Period. The answer lies partly in the attitude toward education and students in the late sixties. The young at that time were called the smartest students in our history, kids who just needed to be let loose to abolish all the evils in society. Such intelligent creatures did not need to be told what to take in school. Many parents agreed: Let Johnny take what he wants.

The pressure on teachers to be permissive was intense. The students had turned introspective; one English teacher called it the who-I-am-and-why-I-hate-my-mother syndrome. A teacher of seventeen years' experience said, "I couldn't get them to do anything academic; all they wanted was *to circle up and play games,*" a phrase she kept repeating throughout the interview. She had in mind a practice of high school and college courses during this period, when teaching called for rearranging chairs into various patterns, the most popular being the circle. But each teacher chose his own geometry. It drove the janitors crazy.

When we talked to English teachers about why they were so eager to install electives, we usually heard the same answers. "I was tired of being hated." "Students disliked the standard surveys of English and American literature." "We weren't doing enough for the bottom half of the class." One teacher said, "Everything we did turned the students off— they didn't like Shakespeare, grammar textbooks, or required courses. They were ruining my good feelings about teaching English." Perhaps an assistant principal in the Middle West put the official school attitude most clearly: "Earlier we were doing nothing for many students. They were hostile to British literature, for instance, and learned nothing from the course. Now they love the little paperbacks they read in courses like Independent Reading and Futuristic Literature. Most students can't understand, and don't need, the so-called literary classics."

In addition, the late sixties were a time for experimentation. If you had an idea that seemed new, whether it was or not, you could get a federal grant. Money came from Washington, and power flowed from the innovators. Yet, for every two teachers in the country who embraced innovation, there was one who did not. Whether, for example, a school adopted electives depended primarily on whether this ratio of two to one obtained in a particular English department. A department with a majority of conservatives was slow to change.

Pressure could, however, be brought to bear on the recalcitrant. If an English department chairman acquired a religious faith in the new grammars, she could see to it that they were taught. The old texts would mysteriously be trucked off to storage; new texts would be bought; and a steady stream of persuasive memos "to keep up with new ideas" would appear in departmental mailboxes. In one southern school, the elective program was the principal's idea; and he pushed it for months until the teachers got tired of resisting and adopted electives. In another school, the teachers came in one day and found that the next term they were going to teach minicourses; the principal had imposed them on the department.

Demands for change were often brought from outside the school but within the administrative system. "Most of our new ideas and changes in curriculum—good or bad—came from outside the school," a midwestern principal told us. In a southwestern school an English teacher said, "In the early seventies, if you taught grammar, you got resistance from the students, but more importantly from the supervisors in the central office." Said the assistant principal in a southeastern school, "Modular scheduling came from the county office; it was forced on us." Superintendents, of course, are generally the most powerful persons in a school system; and if they are pushing change, change will occur.

In addition, powerful influences were at work beyond the limits of school districts. One of these was the accrediting association. There are six associations in the United States, and they see to it that teams of teachers and other experts visit schools periodically to evaluate their programs. In New England, a small high school was criticized by the New England Association of College and Secondary Schools because it did not provide enough "motivation" for students. To solve this problem, the school established electives. In the Midwest, the North Central Association (NCA), possibly the most powerful of the accrediting agencies, was often pointed out to us as the moving force behind change. In late 1976, the NCA made these specific suggestions to a midwestern school: "(1) Provide more electives for eleventh and twelfth graders, for the purpose of satisfying the college-bound and lower-ability students as well as the average and gifted. (2) Buy additional textbooks for composition [even though, we thought, the school is not using the large number it already has in an orderly or consistent fashion]. (3) Give more support to 'media classes.'"

Media study, a rich field for innovators, solves one nagging problem—what to do with the many students who cannot or will not read anything that deserves the name of literature. In some communities, they may form 75 percent of the student body. By "teaching" television, newspapers, car-repair magazines, and movies, students can be kept quiet, occupied, and in school. Such courses have little or nothing to do with grammar, reading, or composition. One department chairman told us, "When we were evaluated by the NCA, we were criticized for not having enough media courses. I was upset because we were trying hard to teach reading and writing."

Still another important influence for change, particularly in the Bad Period, was the federal government. The offices of education launched many experiments in the teaching of grammar and composition, most of which are now forgotten. Supported by money poured into the schools, an army of curricular scientists tinkered and hammered. One principal said he believed that there was a link between these experiments and lowered college-entrance scores; so much confusion was created that the basics were slighted. On the Pacific Coast, another principal stated that over a period of time federal money "encourages educational segregation by creating 'curricular pockets,' such as Black Studies or Career Education." Once you have such pockets established in a school, he added, "the feds pull out and leave you with an inferior program that works badly and tenured teachers using up salary money the regular teachers ought to have."

Hanging over school programs, in all their various forms, is the majestic figure of the law. Today, the courts are a major force in teaching and curricular change. But wherever the law solves one problem in education, it creates half a dozen others. Electives were often established because schools were afraid of lawsuits over the tracking of students. The cure can be worse than the disease. When, in 1976, parents in Tucson, Arizona, wondered where their students' honors classes had gone, the *Arizona Daily Star* sent a reporter out to investigate. An assistant superintendent told the reporter that honors classes cannot be labeled as such because of federal guidelines against racial discrimination. When "ethnic balance" in classes became mandatory, the assistant principal at Tucson High said, the honors classes were done away with. In 1976 Tucson High had a "minority population" of 68 percent.[1]

Even if the courts do not interfere, when high schools have large numbers of minority students, the upper-level (or top-phase) electives tend to disappear because they are not chosen by enough students. School boards will not support a class in chemistry or English composition with only five or six students. In the fall of 1974, a school in the deep south taught five sections of Afro-American Literature, eight of American Literature, and five of Mass Media—the sections averaging at least twenty students apiece. But not taught, because too few students registered for them, were Advanced Grammar, Study of Individual Authors, and World Literature. This school has a 60 percent minority enrollment.

English teachers and school people in general have learned to live, it would seem, with the powers that afflict them from within and without. For the most part, they face them with resignation and occasionally with humor. But one of these powers is regarded nearly everywhere with a dislike that approaches abhorrence. This is what one administrator described to us as "the jackass authority—the college professor who has never taught in high school." Our administrator warmed to his subject: "For a large fee, this professor jets into town with a briefcase full of crazy ideas on mimeograph paper. He gives a workshop to English teachers, some of whom will lap up anything that's weird. A couple days later, he leaves on the plane with an empty briefcase and a bagful of our money. He gave our teachers a shot in the arm, but he did not give us any way to deal with the problems that arise when they try out his ideas." We heard a good deal about the professor with a briefcase on our travels. It is amusing to note that when he was mentioned, gullibility concerning his ideas was assigned to administrators by teachers and to teachers by administrators.

We will return to the role of the professor in English teaching later. At this point, let us consider a question concerning the phase-elective system. Why does it seem destined to last? One reason is that after being modified, it satisfies a number of demands. Teachers like it because it gives variety to what is for many of them an essentially dull job. It also allows teachers to teach their specialty: science fiction, business English, or modern poetry. In many high schools, teachers specialize rather as college professors do, a practice that gives them a sense of importance. Often when we arrived at a school, we were introduced not to an English teacher but to the grammar or reading or American literature teacher.

Students like electives for obvious reasons. The program gives them a sense of being in control of their schooling, together with a way of getting around the harder courses. A department chairman in a Middle Atlantic state said, "The guidance counselors love our film course, which gives them a place to dump the problem students who are always in their office complaining about school." Administrators and school boards approve of the program because it gives them a handy answer to the barrage of criticism they get from the public: "Our school must be doing a good job; it's got something for everybody. If you [parent or student] don't like what you've got, it's your fault. You made the choice."

Such is the ultimate defense of the "cafeteria curriculum": *You* made the choice. We (teachers, administrators, school-board members) can now say to everybody else in America (congressmen, the Department of Health, Education, and Welfare, government lawyers, civil-rights advocates, accrediting associations, scholars in the universities, members of the press, and parents) that the school has done the job. We put a great big plate of goodies before you; how—or whether—you ate them was your affair. The scheme solves the problem of student lack of interest and at the same time shifts the ultimate responsibility for education to the shoulders of those professionally least able to bear it, the students.

But it would be unwise to condemn electives outright. As long as Americans insist on the so-called comprehensive high school, the English elective is not necessarily a bad thing. Various kinds of students must be catered to in any comprehensive institution. And yet certain questions will not go away: How do you get rid of fraudulent electives like Film Study? How do you keep electives from crowding out, as they have already done in many schools, useful courses like British Literature? Bad courses drive out good. In a West Coast school, we found this: *English 340: Pop Culture— Prereq.: English 202, and English 221.* Chaucer, Shakespeare, Pope, and Browning are goners when placed in competition with Paul McCartney and *Rolling Stone.*

Most contemporary high school graduates would not recognize the names of those four poets, last seen in the standard anthologies of twenty or thirty years ago. With only two exceptions, every English department in our sample is now teaching more recent literature than it was a decade ago. Beginning in the late sixties, this practice of teaching the moderns grew out of two convictions. One was that courses had to be "relevant." In a Middle Atlantic state, an older teacher reported that the superintendent brought in a supervisor of English from another city whose mission was "to upgrade the city's English programs for relevance." According to the teacher, the supervisor "wrecked our basic literature programs by establishing minicourse electives that were taught like courses in psychology and sociology."

Many schoolmen who support electives were also convinced that they were failing to do enough for those not college-bound. Accordingly, courses sprouted in the cirriculum that bore names like Advanced Literature of the Outdoorsman (this in a Rocky Mountain state). Such courses were made possible by the spread of the paperback. Parts of the textbook library in an American school often look like the display rack of a drugstore. One finds *All the President's Men, The Greening of America, Little Big Man, Soul on Ice.* Across the aisle, you may see *Mr. Roberts, Inherit the Wind, A Raisin in the Sun, People of the Deer, Brian's Song, Dune, The Inferno, The Iliad.* "We no longer teach textbooks," said a department chairman in the Northwest. "I have a huge inventory of paperbacks—the school board lets us buy anything we want. I feel like a librarian."

The traditional courses in literature during the Bad Period tended to be crowded out by flowering electives and the demand for relevance. *The Iliad* and *The Inferno* are in the paperback library, but they are not being taught very often. In one school's catalogue for registration, the course Literature of the Outdoorsman was next to British Literature, but the second did not fill up and was not given that term. So the British anthology gathered dust on the shelf while a halfdozen paperbacks on hunting and fishing went into vigorous circulation. (When asked, an English teacher said she could not teach anything so difficult as A. B. Guthrie's *The Big Sky* in the Outdoors course. Years ago one used to hear that *Julius Caesar* was difficult for ninth-graders; now we are told that *Lord of the Flies* is too hard for the general run of tenthgraders or that "science fiction is too difficult in vocabulary for many of the students who elect it.")

Americans may come to forget that a traditional literature exists. University English departments have discovered that classes in British literature of the seventeenth, eighteenth, and nineteenth centuries are hard, sometimes impossible, to fill. The university-trained high school teacher is unlikely to teach what she does not know, which may explain occasional odd remarks like the following from an experienced high school teacher: "We are really going to have to start requiring some of the classics—Hawthorne and Stephen Crane." In another school, an experienced teacher referred to "the traditional author, J. D. Salinger." In one handsome suburban school, teachers said, "We do not teach any classics like Mark Twain." This turned out to be an error: *The Mysterious Stranger* could be found in an elective called The Devil in Literature.

Of all the forces at work on a student's training in English, the most important is the teacher. What are high school English teachers like? What are their attitudes? How have they been trained? How good is the work they do?

The majority of English teachers are women. Men can make splendid teachers of the subject, but on the average women are better. For one thing, because English teaching is not considered a manly occupation, many men seem hesitant to undertake teaching as a career. If they have ambition, they tend to do graduate work and get into administration—supposing they stay in education. The presence of many men in a high school English department can usually be accounted for by reasons other than their interest in the profession. Where the salaries are low, there are often no men: the higher the pay, the more men. In those states where the requirements in college hours for teaching English are low, schools hire men who can coach and teach English or social studies as their second assignment.

Perhaps because we live in a university town whose schools have in the past hired a certain number of young, inexperienced English teachers, we had expected to see the same thing elsewhere and thus to find in our sample a fair representation of young teachers recently out of school. We found but few, the average teacher being thirty years old or over. In one large district in a good-sized city, the average

age of high school teachers was fifty, and the average salary, $15,133. Age considered by itself can be misleading, because many women start a family before they go into teaching. We found several teachers in their forties who had no more than four or five years' experience. It was not unusual, by the way, for our sample English departments to be staffed mainly by teachers with five or more years' experience. An "experienced teacher" may be defined as one with five or more years in the high school classroom. The younger teachers—and this is particularly true of those just out of college—are either not getting jobs or get mainly the undesirable ones, particularly in rural or slum schools. We feel no prejudice against rural schools, but we find that many young university-trained English teachers do.

We had also expected to find teachers who were more like our own undergraduate students, among whom can still be found the carefree hippy type. In fifty departments, we saw only one of these, a thirty-year-old speech teacher who admitted to "using slang and fad language and wearing jeans to make students like me." In a number of schools, the teachers we met looked like lady bankers—an impression not belied by shiny new cars on display in the faculty parking lots. Result of unofficial survey in the more prosperous communities: Teacher does not drive to school in a cheap little compact but in an Oldsmobile Cutlass.

In the South, an experienced teacher may be lucky to earn $9,000 a year; in one northern suburban school some teachers were earning over $20,000. Salaries of $14,000–$15,000 are not unusual, but one must consider that in certain communities this is the reward of ten years of experience and two years of graduate work. As a principal told us, "This salary may seem satisfactory, but it does not compare well with the income of some of our own graduates who did not go to college but who at the same age are averaging $25,000 to $30,000 in the business world of this city."

To make ends meet, men teachers may take a second job during the school year. In agricultural areas, farming is a source of income. In a north midwestern school, we were told that "most men here have a second job." One English teacher had been cooking in a steak house four or five nights a week for thirteen years. His wife taught also, and the good life, rather than survival, was his motive. "I like to live well," he said. "I play the stock market, and recently bought myself a golf cart." We spent several hours in the faculty coffee room in this school listening to the men from all departments discussing their second businesses, from farming to carpentry.

Women usually do not take second jobs. And like the men, they do not feel, most of them, that they should carry their jobs home with them. The work day in most schools runs between six and seven hours—from about 8:30 to about 3:00. If you teach five classes, or a total of one hundred and thirty to one hundred and fifty students, and have one period off for preparation and paper grading, you have had a full day. By the end of it, it has been a harder day than the average American making your salary has had. You are probably a married woman and you want to get home and put your feet up for a little while before children and husband arrive to start making demands. A department chairman in New England said, "My teachers are just like other normal people. They have families, children, hobbies, outside interests. When they leave this school, they like to leave school problems, including paper grading, behind them."

Most of the administrators we encountered were satisfied with the performance of their English staff. "We'd like them to give more work in the basics," said one principal, "but we realize that with their loads, we can't ask much more of them. We have teachers who aren't very good, but none who are terrible; and the best two or three are superb." Indeed, the complaints that we heard from every side were not usually about the established staff but about the new teachers just out of college. "They don't know their own field," said one chairman. "I asked this girl if she were going to teach Pepys next week, and she said, 'Who is Pepys?'" Experienced people reserved their strongest expressions of dissatisfaction for the attitude of new teachers toward composition and grammar. "They think it's beneath them to teach the basics," said an older teacher. "Most of them frown on what they call 'dull' vocabulary tests and grammar drill—yet this is the only way to teach these things." One chairman said, "Even if the new teachers wanted to do the basics, most of them couldn't; the universities haven't taught them any grammar and composition. They come in this school and flounder!"

Established departments, particularly the better ones, are so suspicious of new teachers that many of them fill vacancies only by hiring a student teacher of their own that they have watched carefully during her period of training. About the failings of student teachers as a group they will turn purple. A chairman in New England said, "For ten years, new student teachers haven't at all been able to teach grammar and usage; they don't know any practical grammar except by instinct." In a Rocky Mountain state, a teacher said of her recent student teachers, "Sometimes they know no grammar and usage—zero. They can't begin to tell students what to do about writing problems, about what's right and what's wrong." Said an older teacher, "They're full of psychology about teaching, but they don't know how to do it."

Experienced teachers are often much alike, at least on the surface; but their social backgrounds and academic training differ a good deal. Kitty Smith went to a converted teacher's college in an area sometimes described as Ozark country. Mrs. Barbara Jones went to Ohio State; Ted Green to an Ivy League school. Green majored in Latin; Smith in English; Jones in education (she later earned an M.A. in English). Many teachers have had at least one undergraduate course in grammar, and a few had courses in the new grammars. Their training in literature is roughly the same (in quantity, if not quality), consisting of survey courses in English and American literature. They seldom have had work in the history of the English language; of the history of grammar and rhetoric they know nothing (English departments do not, as a rule, give courses in this subject). Unless they have worked on a doctorate, which is rare, they have taken no courses in "philology," as English departments used to classify Anglo-Saxon, Middle English, and so on.

Are you wondering what happened to the bearded and bright-eyed radical teachers who graduated in the late sixties and marched out to save the world from the boredom of grammar and the snobbery of Standard English? When they started teaching, reality overtook most of them. The shock of encountering batches of unwashed, unpleasant, and unteachable students flushed the idealism clean out of their brains and them out of the public schools. Some of them were talented people. Now they repair motorcycles, work in the front office of the Coca-Cola plant, or strive for a Ph.D while supported by a spouse. A few stayed in high school teaching, promising themselves that a social revolution was coming which would sweep love and beauty into the classroom. From among these came the strongest proponents of the elective courses. After a while, the beard began to itch and the wife wanted a house instead of an apartment. Tenure was on the horizon. One day the radical appeared in school all shaved and shiny and wearing a thing that resembled a necktie. The next year he gained tenure and voted to restrict the elective system and to institute a new course in grammar.

Such are teachers viewed in the mass. Viewed as individuals they have, to be sure, the usual peculiarities, some of which carry over into their work. The best of their teaching is superb; the worst makes description not credible. Let us nevertheless try to show one of the worst at work, exactly as he was observed.

The classroom is dirty. The chairs are in disarray: four chairs in a corner, a line of them across the back of the room, another group in the middle, and a group toward the front. Girls sit in front, boys along the back. There are twenty students in the class.

First, the teacher reads announcements. Then he gives a pretest on Conrad's "The Secret Sharer." (A pretest is usually a short quiz, often of the objective type, to test whether the students have read the assigned material.) Since he does not monitor the test, some of the students discuss the answers and some cheat. Each student takes his test to the teacher, disturbing those who are trying to work. Two boys come in late during the test, sneering at the teacher, who ignores them.

After a pretest, the teacher asks questions, in most cases answering them himself because the students do not volunteer readily. He never calls on a student. All that is said by the class—with the exception of wisecracks from the back of the room—comes from two boys and one girl. When irrelevancies are uttered, the teacher does not try to exclude them. All comments are treated as if equally valuable in the analysis of the story. Throughout this part of the period, there is constant talking in various parts of the room; at no time are all the students paying attention to the discussion; two boys read magazines throughout. Some students do not have the textbook with them. Those who have their books do not open them and refer to the text when the teacher asks them to. Toward the end of the period, the teacher gives up and asks the students to study the next day's assignment. Four or five do; the rest do as they please.

Now for a look at an excellent teacher in action. She is working in an old school, built in 1927. Her classroom is dingy but well lighted, and the chairs are neatly arranged in a horseshoe half-circle, with the teacher's desk at the open end. The students seat themselves randomly, except for those who have ties of romance or friendship. No student comes in late; everyone is seated when the teacher arrives. When she starts her class, the talking stops.

She begins with unfinished business, handing back papers and answering questions about them. Next she reviews the assignments for the several days ahead, reminding students of deadlines for the reading and writing assignments. Then she begins the work for the day, a discussion of *The Stranger* by Albert Camus, before which comes a pretest. After grumbling a bit, the students take the ten-minute quiz; she monitors it by walking around the room. (One sign of a good teacher: she stays on her feet.) At her signal, all students hand in the test at the same time.

She goes over the test with them and then begins the discussion period, during which students raise questions or make comments that are suggested by both the work and the pretest. During the discussion she accepts volunteers who wish to answer questions. From the response given, she frames new or related questions, sometimes asking students to qualify or elaborate their earlier remarks.

She refers continually to the text, to the evidence of the work. She never answers her own questions and makes an effort to include all students, calling on them as necessary. When talking breaks out, she stops it quickly and firmly.

By the time the period is over, she and her students have discussed all the pretest questions and have introduced a number of other issues relevant to *The Stranger*. The class work ends only when the bell rings.

This teacher's technique is obvious, you say? Yes, in the same way, for example, that the technique of the professional actor is obvious. There are only so many ways to ask a question in the classroom or to move upstage and deliver a speech. The point is to perform as economically as possible and move on to something else: leave art to the artists, of whom there are only a few in any generation. Most of us must be content merely to be competent.

Yet a new teacher may find it difficult to learn how to be competent. It is likely that the last good teaching of the language she experienced for any length of time occurred in high school, and there is nature's law of amnesia operating in the mind of a neophyte: she will not be able to remember the method of her own successful teachers. (No one understands why this law works so efficiently, but it does.) In college, her English department gave her a bumbling teaching assistant for freshman English and a course in transformational grammar when she was a junior. Her professor in English Teaching Methods—a course usually taught in the College of Education—did not greet with warmth the idea of what educationists call, in their immaculately illiterate jargon, the structured classroom. That is, organizing, or structuring, a piece of learning is forbidden. We heard the tale of an experienced substitute teacher, a woman who had decided to return to college to earn her secondary certificate. When she gave a sample lesson in her methods class, analyzing a paragraph of professional modern prose for the purpose of showing how the sentences were made and connected, the professor went into a rage. "I thought he was going to have a heart attack right there," the woman said. "He told us that we should *never* teach in this 'structured' way; that we should use the student's own work for analysis, not the work of professionals."

Let us return to our two contrasted teachers, the good one and the bad. In a world where education is valued, it hardly seems possible that the bad teacher could survive. Yet survive he did through his probationary years, until he achieved tenure. His weaknesses were known all along, but since he had not pinched any girls' bottoms, stolen any lunch money, or come to school drunk, no particular objections were made to his being kept on. The school he works in is a bad one, one of the weakest in our sample, in a university town.

Our good teacher works in a school that has a firm curriculum with no electives, a strong administration, a regular program of teacher supervision, and a sense of educational purpose. None of these are found in the poorer school, which has some good teachers in most subjects, but not its due share. If they can, teachers leave this place, either by resignation, early retirement, or ascent into administration. We should mention that the inferior work of the bad teacher was discovered by visitors to his class who were not connected with the school system. Supervisors had failed in their duty to him, the public, and the children.

We may seem to have strayed from our original subject, the confusion in present-day high school English teaching. Everything mentioned so far, from curricular change to the uncertain quality of instruction, contributes to this confusion, as well as to instability in the schools. Many teachers face almost constant change. As the "enlisted men" of a system, they are required to do its main work: keeping discipline, "bookkeeping" a paperback library, teaching the reading of simple sentences to eighteen-year-olds, and a host of other duties. They also endure considerable variation in leadership, because the officer class of administrators in schools is notoriously unstable.

This is readily understood. Administrators, being ambitious, move fairly often. Particularly is this true of the junior executives—guidance counselors, assistant principals, associate superintendents—the people who really run the schools. The senior executives (i.e., principals and superintendents), like the good generals they are, prefer to operate behind the lines where no bullets are whistling. It is amusing to find, in many schools of any size, an assistant principal for discipline; and it is he, not the principal, who is involved with policemen and lawyers and expulsion hearings and angry parents. When the assistant principal for discipline has a chance to move five hundred miles to another state and become a real principal, he naturally jumps at the opportunity.

On many occasions, we would put questions to administrators only to be told, "I don't know the answer to that question, this is just my first or second year here. You'd better check with the teachers." We were amazed at how little is likely to be known, or recorded systematically, about the past of a school. You can talk to three teachers, one librarian, an assistant principal, and two guidance counselors, and still not get an accurate account of what was done about an issue or problem. In some instances nothing was done because there was nobody there to do it. A junior administrator resigns and leaves the state; mail addressed to him piles up unread; his desk gathers dust; and no one takes over his duties—unless people like ourselves show up and ask questions. We have stood for hours in empty offices, shifting from one foot to another while a patient secretary from another office hunts through unfamiliar files for a piece of information that our vanished administrator "must have had here somewhere."

The known history of an American high school is commonly little more than a year or two in length. What used to be a "school community" (formed by a loose coalition of parents, students, teachers, administrators, and laymen) has largely disappeared, in part because lasting, self-defined communities have largely disappeared. By itself, the trend to bigger, comprehensive high schools has caused the dissolution of identifiable school communities. In the modern school, few or no historical notes are kept; the professionals do not remember how a program was carried out three years ago or who was teaching World Lit then. Everyone from the janitor to the guidance counselor tends to go his own way. It is bad form to pry into another's business. More important, schools are run according to the first Law of Maladministration: Don't act—react. If you don't do a thing, you can't be blamed for it. But when anyone comes sniffing around wanting information, give it to him if you can do so without being blamed.

As a spectacular example of this state of things, consider our experience with the college entrance tests—the American College Test (ACT) and the Scholastic Aptitude Test (SAT), given respectively by the American College Testing Program and the Educational Testing Service. Since we were interested in any relationship between English teaching and the decline in both the ACT and SAT test scores, we wrote ahead to most of the schools on our route, asking them to have these scores ready for us for the period 1965–75. Administrators said they would help us in this and other matters; one cannot fault them for being uncooperative. Of the fifty schools we visited, few could provide the requested scores. Of those schools stressing the ACT test, ten had no test scores or could not find them when we were there; thirteen had scores for 1969–75; one had scores for 1965–75; nine had significant gaps in scores for 1969–75; and one refused to give any scores. Of those schools stressing the SAT test, six had too few scores to be significant; five had scores for 1965–75; and five had scores, but the number of students taking the test was insignificant (three of these schools used a state college-entrance test).

The important period for the test scores was that between the school years of 1965 and 1975. The great furor over declining scores occurred when it was announced in the 1974–75 school year that for a decade American students had been doing progressively worse on the college-entrance tests. Dozens of stories in newspapers, magazines, and professional journals followed, "explaining" the decline in scores. Most of the schools we visited were disturbed by the drop and trying "to do something about it."

Yet as the figures given above indicate, two years after the testing services had sounded the warning, only six schools in our sample had sufficient information to evaluate their own programs and scores in relation to national trends. But despite the lack of this information most of them were busily changing curricula and teaching methods—frequently operating, it would appear, in the dark. Of our fifty schools, only ten had prepared a report to the public about their situation in regard to the scores, but that was usually done for a particular year, to show that the school's scores, even though they had gone down, were still better than the national mean. Individual cases were marked by comedy. In a Rocky Mountain state, a former principal had thrown away all the scores, and the curriculum supervisor had no idea what they were. In a large southwestern school, the guidance counselor stated that his scores were declining, but he was able to find the figures for only two years. (How could he say they were "declining"?) In a Middle Atlantic state, the chairman of the English department had no notion of how his students were doing on the tests. In New England, an able principal—at least, he appeared able to us, and his school was excellent—did not even know which test his school used. In a southern school we were greeted with, "We don't know where the scores are, or even if we have ever had them."

The English department chairman of another school in the South remarked; "On the basis of the declining scores, we have had big pressure from the school board to change our curriculum." But no office in his school had a record of any scores at all, so neither the board nor administrators and teachers had evidence with which to act on the question. High up in New England, a pleasant and seemingly well-informed young chief guidance counselor gave us a short, but detailed and convincing, speech on why the scores in his school were going down. "Well, let's take a look at them," we said. But he did not know where they were or, as it turned out, what they were. When they were finally discovered, we all learned together that the school had five consecutive sets of verbal SAT scores going through 1974; they showed a low point in 1972 but a definite upward trend in the three sets for 1972, 1973, and 1974. Said the counselor, "I guess it's obvious I haven't looked at these lately."

The history of most schools, then, is being erased nearly as fast as it is being made, a situation hazardous for all concerned, including the investigator. How does he—or those in charge—find facts upon which to base a reasonable interpretation of conditions in the system? Everyone says that curricula have changed in the past decade or so, but where are the curriculum guides of 1967? Gone, most of them, with the wind. It is commonplace to say that student writing is not as good as it used to be, but where are the student papers of the past? Long since incinerated. (In England, test questions and answers and national scores are available back to 1900, and in some cases beyond.) We had been three and a half months on the road before we found an experienced teacher who had actually kept sample papers from the years she had taught. We were so surprised we nearly fell off our chairs.

There is yet another element that adds to the confusion surrounding high school English teaching—the sociopolitical pressure that schoolmen constantly feel. All of them feel it, from the superintendent down to the lowliest clerk and teacher's aide. Senior administrators are so fearful that they commonly refuse to issue any order which might activate one of the pressure groups multiplying within and without the institution like some dreadful outer-space fungus. "There's a new bunch around here every week," said one principal. In our interviews we heard about one group for discipline and one against it; one group for back to basics and one for remedial English (these two may or may not be the same group); one for the teaching of Latin and one for doing away with all foreign-language courses except Spanish; one for bidialectal teaching and one against it; one against the New Math; one for testing and one against testing; one for career education and one against career education; one against "dirty" books in the school and one for the "students' right to read."

Ah, those rights! A midwestern state department of education published a bulletin on the rights of students but failed to mention any of their responsibilities. When the principal of a school pointed this out to the department, he received no enlightenment, not even, he said, "the courtesy of a reply." Since the bulletin presumably had the force of law, the principal was understandably concerned. "The law," said W. S. Gilbert ironically, "is the true embodiment of everything that's excellent." It would take more than Gilbertian irony to comment adequately upon the chaos that the idea of rights has created in the school. An administrator cannot move for fear of infringing a person's rights. If he "allows" girls to be attacked in the restroom by other girls who are after their lunch money, the victims' right to be free from fear is infringed; if he hires an adult female guard to police the toilets, the same girls' right to privacy has been infringed. Furthermore, if the guard is white, black, brown, or yellow, the rights of girls not of that color will be infringed. So the administrator removes the guard—and the door to the restroom—on the theory that without the door any yells from right-deprived and money-robbed girls can be more easily heard. This story is not made up.

Every school system has its great chain of being. At the top, somewhat uneasily, sits the superintendent; at the bottom, somewhat anxiously, the teacher. The superintendent can send an order to the assistant superintendent, who can send it to the curriculum supervisor, who can send it to the principal, who can send it to the assistant principal, who can send it to the English department chairman, who can send it to the English teacher, who cannot send it to anybody. Whether she obeys the order is a separate question.

Almost every person in the chain can avoid at least some of the pressure on him by refusing to become a target for any group or individual. One can shift responsibility: "You'll have to talk to the guidance counselors; I'm really not up on testing practices." Or one simply disappears from the scene, as a principal did in our city a few years ago every time there was a student disturbance. Teachers find it more difficult to evade a responsibility or disappear and hence are more vulnerable to pressure.

If teachers give many low grades, they may hear from an administrator, perhaps by means of an official letter stating that "you were out of line in your grading last term." In some schools, failing a student is sure to bring a comment. One teacher in our state said, "Our superintendent made the remark in faculty meeting that 'a failing student is a failing teacher.' We all got the message." Department chairmen may be asked to give directions: "Don't you think that a book report every six weeks is too much?" That teacher stopped assigning book reports.

The elective system has greatly influenced the way English teachers feel about their performance as professionals. With declining enrollments and schools closing, they sense that the way to stay employed is to be popular. And, to a considerable degree, given even a modified elective program, they are involved in a popularity contest, to lose which, for the nontenured teacher, can mean to lose the job.

The pressure from parents is both continual and broadly applied. Where, at one time, a teacher might receive only an occasional outburst from a parent who felt that Johnny had been unfairly graded or unreasonably detained after school, she is now led to believe that Johnny can do generally what he wants. He can choose his own courses, teachers, grades, and behavior. "The pressure we get," said a teacher of long experience, "is for the kids to do whatever they please. If they want to cut class to work in the afternoon, that is just fine with parents. Our course schedules are made out for the convenience of students and parents, not for educational purposes." Occasionally, parents go to extraordinary lengths to preserve their children from education. We visited a school in what teachers referred to as the Golden Ghetto. "This is a very prosperous community," said the English chairman. "Psychiatry and 'learning problems' are all the rage. Parents can take a kid to a local clinic and for $200 get a diagnosis of dyslexia—*you* could get one for $250. So they get the pressure off their kid for learning to read."

Increasingly, students work to support cars and social activities. A sociologist could write a popular book on the effect of fast-food chains on American civilization. These and other businesses support the social aspirations of hundreds of thousands of teenagers, who might better be spending their time in school or at play. A favorite slogan of the great American movement for the free public high school has been: Keep them off the streets and in school. But who will now keep them in school? In California, a high school gets its full share of state aid—$7 a day for each student if he or she is present for one period. "Students can come here for a few minutes and leave," said a California principal. We visited a midwestern school, quite a good one, we thought, which sends over 70 percent of its students to college. There, a student can cut any number of classes in certain courses and still pass. "It depends on the teacher," said a guidance counselor. "Some teachers care and some don't. In Creative Writing, a student last year could miss forty sessions and still pass. But not in Pre-College Composition, because the teacher wouldn't stand for it." For a time, this school had a rule that students would be suspended from a class after ten unexcused absences, "but the parents wouldn't let us make it stick."

The most steady demand for permissiveness comes from the students themselves. The average teacher sees about one hundred and fifty of them a day. Some cannot read and many more prefer not to—the commonest request for class activity being, as we often heard, for movies, film strips, and slides. Honors students decline to study *Walden* or *Crime and Punishment.* "Ten years ago," said a teacher, "I could assign *Ivanhoe;* now I couldn't even get students to start that book." Said another teacher, "It's very hard to teach writing; even the better students aren't much interested in it—and student interest controls what you teach." More, it controls both how and if one teaches. When a school "meets the needs of students," as the cliché has it, students have gained significant control of the academic side of school life. "Our curriculum," said a teacher, "is what the students will tolerate. Here, we are afraid of required courses, because the students wouldn't like them." A student will tell his teacher in various ways how much he will stand. He may interrupt in class, sneer, threaten to call his parents, complain to the guidance counselor, shout, throw books on the floor, keep up a constant stream of criticism about the class work—and threaten, threaten, threaten. Out of one hundred and fifty students, it takes only a few such to reduce a teacher to gibbering. In a very few days a single student can do it quite satisfactorily.

It would be wrong to think that the description of these attitudes and tactics is exaggerated. We ourselves have seen administrators, parents, and students put pressure on teachers; and in our forty years of combined experience, we have had every variety put on us. We made one tedious evening of driving on a desert highway pass more quickly by recalling the villains of our professional history and their various menaces—from that of the full professor of law and his wife who recently threatened Charlene at an open meeting because in her high school class she was giving "low grades" on papers (*B*'s and *C*'s), to the college president two decades ago who harassed Arn for a year. He berated him in his office, hauled him before a member of the board of the university, even managed to get him investigated by a committee of the legislature. Arn's offense? He had publicly objected to the president's changing the grades of athletes so that they could stay eligible.

Teachers have invented a multitude of devices to deal with the demands made upon them. The best is to get out of teaching entirely, if possible. We were puzzled by the large number of English teachers we encountered who were earning degrees in counseling, administration, or librarianship until it was pointed out to us that with advanced degrees in English they would be condemned to the classroom forever. "After seventeen years," said a teacher in a wealthy community in the South, "I can't wait to get out."

If information on teaching practices or student achievement is asked for, teachers can plead the so-called Buckley Amendment, which was designed to keep student records private. If in conservative communities a parent objects to certain books being read, the teachers can require that each student bring a reading release form to school. Or they can assign readings by author, not by title, since they have learned that parents react to the title *1984* but not to the name George Orwell and to *Catcher in the Rye* but not to J. D. Salinger. They can join a union and, if the union is strong enough, stay in the classroom but retire from the battlefield, since the union will become their champion. "We have the union," said an experienced teacher, "to keep the administration, parents, and board from running right over us." He made no mention of money considerations, which might suggest that money came last in his list of union benefits.

No matter how strong a union may be or how cleverly teachers learn to avoid constraints placed upon them, they may still find themselves powerless in the politics of the classroom. One cannot teach British literature if the class does not "fill" with students who voted for it in the elective system and the course is not offered. (The same is true of honors courses.) If a school has to start at 7:00 in the morning and close at 1:00 because citywide bussing has been decreed and busses have to run all day long, there is little the teacher can do about absent or sleepy children. "I learned there are some I'd better not wake up." The responsibility for maintaining attendance in most schools has been shifted for political reasons to the shoulders of the teacher, but she has been given little genuine authority to keep students in school.

When the American high school works at all—that is, when it performs its function as a teaching institution—it does so at great and ponderous effort. For the school is a large, enfeebled creature, set upon by every sharp-toothed carnivore where it ranges, and so confused by its tormentors that at times it may barely remember what it lives for. So it blunders on toward a vaguely perceived destination amidst a disorder only partly of its own making.

For the five months of our trip, in a hundred and fifty motel rooms, we used to ponder a question: What keeps the beast on its feet? We saw schools that ought to have been dead long ago still gamely going through the motions of education and sometimes doing a good deal more useful work than could have been expected of them in their condition. For keeping the schools alive, we can thank a relatively small number of teachers and administrators who struggle on in spite of the authors of their confusion. Another question: Why are some schools free of the worse sorts of confusion and bad teaching, even though their histories up to the early 1970's are not noticeably different from those of schools that are failing? At least four schools in our sample do so good a job that they might be recommended as models of secondary teaching. Two of these were described in the preceding chapter.

We concluded that aside from luck, which is certainly a factor, the better schools have one thing in common: a community determined to educate its children. This determination is translated into action when townspeople elect a school board that will pick an equally determined superintendent. Then, if through the administrative hierarchy—including, most importantly, a good principal and department chairman—the superintendent sees to it that this determination is made known to the teachers, educational disorder is averted or cleaned up.

There are many school systems that lack a determined superintendent. The quality of the school then depends mainly on the tenaciousness and determination of the principal, who provides leadership and gives authority to his department chairmen. We often have heard a principal refer to top administrators "uptown" or in "the central office," in criticism of their failure to support his efforts toward a better program or educational environment. In a fully integrated system in the deep south, in one instance, the central office was actually fighting the high school principal in his efforts to maintain discipline and keep the students in school. Frequently, parents will not support a principal like this until he threatens to resign. When they realize that he helps to keep their children in school, they will go to his defense. In the case just cited, the very parents whose children were being disciplined and who were complaining to the superintendent ended up supporting the principal they had vigorously tried to remove.

To sum up, the key to the good teaching of English is not to be found necessarily in class size; the age, experience, or training of the teacher; teachers' salaries; the size of the school; the type of neighborhood (excepting most slum areas); or the sophistication, wealth, or size of the community. It is possible for a poor black child in Mississippi to get better training in the language than it is for a doctor's child in a sparkling new school in the glamorous Southwest. The main key is the public's determination and support and a firm administration up and down the line. To be included, perhaps, is a strong antipathy, on the part of everyone concerned, to bad ideas—particularly those peddled by college professors who themselves have never taught in the schools.

4☆
Bad Ideas About Language

The decline of American English in the population at large has many causes, most of them complex. They range from the decay of culture to partly accidental changes in speech patterns. Prominent among the cultural causes one can point to a particular body of linguistic theory in this century that has influenced thought and language in our society. Dictionary making has been affected, as have school textbooks and the teaching of English itself. What your child learns— or does not learn—about his native tongue in school may be to a considerable extent controlled by bad (that is, unrealistic and unworkable) ideas about language and the teaching of it.

Bad ideas about English did not arise overnight, nor did they become a force in our linguistic philosophy without a struggle. Indeed, America in the twentieth century has seen a conflict over words longer than the Wars of the Roses, and the issues of that conflict still have the power to inflame passions. The most important of these issues, put in question form, are these: What is language? Is it speech? If so, when is it speech? What is good usage? What do we mean by *good English* (or *good grammar*)? Who are the scholars who will supply the rules?

All of these are related to the question of authority, which until a half-century or so ago was not a difficult question. Up to that time, a school teacher, an editor, or a minister of the gospel—in short, any person considered by the general public to be better educated than the average—might set himself up in America as an authority on language. In the United States, *language* usually meant the English language first. The scholarly authorities might or might not be professors of English. If they were experts in Old Norse and other mysteries and wore beards of sufficient grandeur, they were probably called philologists, a term of considerable breadth. John M. Manly, a great American philologist, was one who took the broad view. When asked about the meaning of philology he answered, "It's life." [1]

Such definitions, however effective in an epigrammatic way, are anathema to the scientific temper. Thus, it is not surprising to discover that when philology went modern and scientific and began to call itself *linguistics*, the vital definitions of the new discipline became much narrower. The complexity of modern linguistic definitions can be shown clearly by a comparison. In 1913, George Lyman Kittredge, the great Shakespearean scholar, and F. E. Farley published a grammar text in which they defined *grammar* as "the science which treats of the forms and the constructions of words." [2]

By 1954, the linguist W. Nelson Francis found it necessary to believe that *grammar* had three meanings: "Grammar 1, a form of behavior; Grammar 2, a field of study, a science; and Grammar 3, a branch of etiquette." [3] Francis defined Grammar 2 as "the branch of linguistic science which is concerned with the description, analysis, and formulization of formal language patterns." [4] As these definitions indicate, the "new grammar," as it can be called, has evolved into a highly technical affair with many subspecialties. It resounds with important terms like *structuralism, transformationalism, ethnolinguistics, dialectology,* and *phonemics.*

Although the terms *old grammar* and *new grammar* imply the existence of trends, for some persons and in some instances the terms are inaccurate. The old grammarian belonged usually to a relatively conservative tradition. But the description of him as a fire-breathing reactionary was largely an invention of certain modern linguists, usually of the "structural" school. The new grammarians considered their work "new" and diametrically opposed to the work of the older authorities. (Many important theoretical linguists, it is necessary to point out, had little or nothing to say about the war over words, for they had their own work to do.) The majority of new grammarians were involved with "English education"—that is, with teacher training, curriculum revision, and the writing of textbooks. Such activities influence millions of our countrymen. When the new grammarians became involved with the making of dictionaries, many more Americans were influenced.

At first, professors of the proliferating new grammar found the going rather rough. Many of them worked in English departments where they were viewed with distaste if not with horror. So they set out to prove to the public and to English teachers everywhere that the old grammarians were wrong in their view of language. The scholarly journals rang with denunciations of the old grammarians, who were called "purists," "prescriptivists," "authoritarians," and "antiscientists." In 1933, for example, the influential linguist Leonard Bloomfield wrote rather grimly that "discrimination of elegant or 'correct' speech is a by-product of certain social conditions. . . . Strangely enough, people without linguistic training devote a great deal of effort to futile discussions of this topic without progressing to the study of language, which alone could give them the key."[5]

Other new grammarians joined the attack in order to discredit what they called the "prescriptive" or "conventional" attitude of the old grammarian. For example, Robert Pooley wrote, "Eighteenth-century theories of language resulted in attitudes and specific rules concerning usage which became fixed and arbitrary in nineteenth-century schoolbooks, and which still persist in the textbooks of today in total disregard for the objective facts of English usage."[6] This writer concluded:

> With the growth of a science of linguistics, interest centered upon usage itself, leading to wordy and violent controversies in which the terms "good" and "bad" English became prominent. This controversy is seen undiminished at the close of the century. But from it two clear positions evolve, which may be identified and carried over into the discussion of the twentieth century. The one . . . hold[s] that language contains a certain innate or, "natural" fitness or correctness which neither authority nor custom can gain-say. The other . . . see[s] language as an objective phenomenon, controlled by, or rather dependent upon, the usage of all who speak it. *There is, of course, no compromise between these two positions.*[7] [Italics added.]

The idea of "no compromise" was picked up by, among others, Professor C. C. Fries, who was perhaps the most influential of the new grammarians. In 1940, he wrote a strong attack on what he called the "conventional point of view [which] assumes not only that there is a correctness in English language as absolute as that in elementary mathematics but also that the measures of this correctness are very definite rules." Fries continued, "From this, the 'conventional point of view,' the problem of the differences in our language practice is a very simple one. Only two kinds of forms or usage exist—correct forms and mistakes."[8]

The only trouble with such statements about the "conventional point of view" is that they were not true. Most of the important authorities in the eighteenth and nineteenth centuries had recognized that usage was king. In his great *Philosophy of Rhetoric* (1776), George Campbell wrote, "It is not the business of grammar, as some critics seem preposterously to imagine, to give law to the fashions which regulate our speech." These fashions, he continued, "no sooner obtain and become general, than they are laws of the language, and the grammarian's only business is to note, collect, and methodize them."[9] A few years after Campbell (1783), the important rhetorician Hugh Blair wrote that "no grammatical rules have sufficient authority to control the firm and established usage of language. Established custom, in speaking and writing, is the standard to which we must at last resort for determining every controverted point in language and style."[10] And by 1913 the old grammarians Kittredge and Farley are found saying, "Grammar does not enact laws for the conduct of speech. Its business is to ascertain and set forth those customs of language which have the sanction of good usage. If good usage changes, the rules of grammar must change."[11]

True, when constructing practical rules on usage for students to follow, many of the old grammarians were rather more prescriptive than the moderns. This attitude sprang from the desire to teach mastery of the rudiments. But in usage theory the old grammar was surprisingly liberal.

It is evident that in their campaign to displace the old grammarians as authorities on language, the new grammarians tended to be somewhat cavalier in their handling of expert opinion. The period from 1850 to 1900 was notable for the publication of excellent books on rhetoric and usage, but authorities such as Barrett Wendell, John Hart, John Genung, and Adams Sherman Hill seldom appear in the accounts of the new grammarians, probably because the older men were customarily enlightened in their theories of usage and consequently could not have provided targets for the new grammarians' attacks.

Another device that the new grammarians used to discredit their opponents was the "science ploy," which associated new linguistic theories with perhaps the most magical idea in modern times: inductive experimental science.

One writer remarked, typically, of "the laws of the science that studies all speech—linguistics."[12] Another new grammarian remarked that an "ideal" grammar should be "logically defensible in the same way that a chemical analysis is logically defensible."[13]

Most significant for educators was the advice from still another new grammarian that the teacher "will have to divorce the study and teaching of 'correct' usage from the study and teaching of grammar. This means that in usage he must follow the general principles of modern scientific language study. If the study of grammar as an intellectual discipline is to be included in a curriculum (and the curriculum maker must decide whether it is or is not), then the course must be different from what passes for grammar today. Conventional formal grammar, which is an eclectic application of certain rules of Latin grammar to arbitrarily selected segments of English morphology and syntax, must give way to a thorough-going inductive study of the English language. The traditional superstitious identification of the 'rules' of English grammar with the 'rules' of a mythical 'good English' must go."[14]

The argument over authority in usage thus became a black-and-white affair. The old "conventional point of view" was all black and all wrong; the new "scientific point of view" was all white and all right; and there could be "no compromise" between the two positions. Most Americans who cared about the subject at all, and this included most English teachers, came to believe that the rhetoricians and grammarians of yesteryear were so witlessly prescriptive that they blanched upon hearing *ain't* and fainted dead away when confronted by a split infinitive. The straw-man technique has seldom been better handled.

By the decade of the 1950's the new grammarians were firmly established as the major authorities on language. Their views were everywhere consulted, even in dictionary making—notably in the revision of the huge Webster, Third Edition. They taught courses on linguistics in the great universities, which sponsored their "institutes," where the faith was vigorously promulgated. They wrote a tremendous number of books and articles, which they themselves reviewed. A new grammarian was elected president of the National Council of Teachers of English (NCTE), the most powerful body of English teachers in the nation. The National Council of Teachers of English is a giant organization of about forty thousand members, 70 percent of whom are in the public schools. It calls itself "the world's largest subject-matter association." The day-by-day running of the organization, centered in our home city of Champaign-Urbana, is controlled by a relatively small group of theorists and college professors who travel from place to place delivering their latest notions of right thinking. The public school teachers can only stand and wait for the next version. Though teachers may control the council at the state level (each state has its own NCTE affiliate), policy is ordinarily set at headquarters. And from headquarters comes the never-ending stream of publicity and propaganda on language and English teaching.

The council itself put its official stamp on the new grammar:

> The National Council of Teachers of English supports the scientific study of the English language, and, realizing the importance of the results of that study in freeing our teaching from wasteful and harmful practices, recommends that in the training of teachers, both prospective and in service, opportunities be provided to acquaint English teachers with the principles, methods, results, and applications of modern linguistic science. Furthermore, the National Council of Teachers of English believes that the schools should teach those forms of the English language which sound descriptive research has shown to be the practice of Standard English in the United States.[15]

The old grammarians had usually considered language as mainly a means of communication. One spoke or wrote in order to tell another person his thoughts. "Language," wrote George Campbell in 1776, "is the sole channel through which we communicate our knowledge and discoveries to others, and through which the knowledge and discoveries of others are communicated to us."[16] In 1933, Leonard Bloomfield, the dean of American new grammarians, made these typical statements: "Writing is not language, but merely a way of recording language by means of visible marks." "The only useful generalizations about language are inductive [i.e., scientific] generalizations." The linguist "observes all speech-forms impartially."[17]

Such statements made by linguists—and the ones quoted are typical of hundreds made by them—are remarkable in three ways. First, they limit language to speech. Second, they imitate the colorless attitude and impartial jargon of science. Third, in their scientific neutrality they imply that value judgments on language are mainly superfluous to its study. From such typical premises of the new grammar were drawn certain conclusions. For example, since language is speech and since speech obviously is not the same everywhere, it follows that, as a linguistic rule, language is forever changing. Now if change is a law of language, correctness is nothing more than what people are saying at a particular time and place.

The new grammarians felt, or pretended to feel, that they were living in a hostile world. Perhaps this fact explains why they allowed a number of their supporters to treat such premises as we quoted—which are really no more than hypotheses—as laws handed down on tablets. Thus, the new grammatical Pentalogue approved by the National Council of Teachers of English:

1.   Language changes constantly;
2.   Change is normal;

3. Spoken language is the language;
4. Correctness rests upon usage;
5. All usage is relative.[18]

The Pentalogue was so important to the controversy that it deserves a few paragraphs of analysis.

(1) *Language changes constantly;* and (2) *Change is normal.* Language does change—erratically. Even in the spoken language, rates of change vary so much that it is difficult to generalize. English is changing less now than it did at times during the Middle Ages. And in given periods, parts of the language change rapidly while others do not. As Professor Sheridan Baker remarks, the whole matter is vastly more complex than we have been led to believe: "Apparently stasis is just as normal, natural, and constant as change; apparently the two co-exist."[19]

(3) *Spoken language is the language.* This is a curious statement, which seems to imply that books do not exist and have no influence. Concerning English alone, one might consider the great effect of the King James Bible on the speech and writing of millions of men and women in the past three centuries. What of the dozens of echoes from Shakespeare, a few of which one hears even on the lips of semiliterate college freshmen? Shakespeare has survived in written form. What of the influence of writing upon writing, as in Melville's Captain Ahab, who speaks in a parody of King Lear? To take a different tack, if spoken language is the language, what are we to do with the political and philosophical documents of the past that have exerted enormous influence in their written forms? What of Plato's *Republic,* Aquinas's *Summa Theologica,* Marx's *Das Kapital,* Hitler's *Mein Kampf,* or the Constitution of the United States? If these are not "language," what are they?

(4) *Correctness rests upon usage;* and (5) *All usage is relative.* To the declaration that all usage is relative, one must

ask, Relative to what? Similarly, to the statement that correctness rests upon usage, one must ask, Whose usage? The old grammarians were very clear: "*Usage governs language. There is no other standard. By usage*, however, is meant the *practice of the best writers and speakers*, not merely the habits of the community in which we chance to live." Thus Professor Kittredge and his coauthors in a textbook dated 1907.[20] Nowadays this appeal to the "best" writers and speakers is vaguely reproved as "authoritarian." But nothing concrete is offered in its place, ignoring the fact that people *want to know*—about language as about diet, astrophysics, or education, in all of which there are recognized authorities. Some usage is better than others. The usage of a longshoreman is probably better than that of a college president if the longshoreman is Eric Hoffer and the president is a Doctor of Education, but that is because Hoffer is a writer who has thought about the problems of writing. The judgment of "better" or "best" in usage refers to the quality of the writing and speaking, not to the authority's place in the social scale.

Until 1961, the battle over language, "science," correctness, and the other items of the new faith seldom strayed outside the scholarly journals. But in that year a book came out which brought the whole affair into the open—*Webster's Third New International Dictionary, Unabridged. Webster's Third*, as it is called, embodied the new dispensation, so that by its advertising and distribution, large numbers of educated Americans could see and judge the results. They did not like what they saw. "Anarchy in Language" said a headline in the *Chicago Sun-Times. Library Journal* suggested that "to serve their users adequately most libraries will need both 2d and 3d editions." The *American Bar Association Journal* said of the *Third:* "A serious blow has recently befallen the cause of good English. . . . The most serious indictment of the new dictionary . . . is that it has utterly abdicated any role as judge of what is good English usage." In a directive issued to the staff of the *New York Times*, Theodore M. Bernstein stated that *Times* editors "have decided without a dissent to continue to follow *Webster's Second Edition* for spelling and usage. *Webster III* will be the authority only for new, principally scientific, words."[21] Public irritation with the *Third* crossed ideological lines. For what must have been the first time in their history, the *National Review* and the *New Republic* agreed—that the new dictionary was flawed.

The publishers of *Webster's Third* were caught seriously off guard. They had planned the work on the new theory and had come to believe that the issues dividing the new and old grammarians had been settled. Philip B. Gove, editor of the *Third*, wrote shortly after publication, "Although some resistance remains, acceptance of the basic tenets of this new science is hardly any longer a matter of opinion." Gove quoted the Pentalogue, paid special homage to the god of Change, decried the type of "best usage" in *Webster's Second*, and said that lexicography "should have no traffic with guesswork, prejudice, or bias or with artificial notions of correctness and superiority. It must be descriptive and not prescriptive." He stated, "An essential requirement for determining best usage is that it be actual genuine usage of such frequency as to be indisputably prevailing. The means, already mentioned, are now available for finding out pretty accurately what that kind of best usage is. What cannot be heard live on radio and television can be recorded on tape and listened to over and over again. Equally important, the sound of words in running speech can be heard over and over again, to satisfy another basic requirement of genuine usage."[22]

To confuse *actual* or *genuine usage* with *best usage* is heedless enough when pronunciation is at stake, but it is evident that *Webster's Third* adopted the same criterion to de-

cide the meaning and creation of words. "Each year," wrote
the publishers in an advertising pamphlet, "brings the development of new techniques and new ideas. . . . Children of
today use easily hundreds of words and meanings not
present in the vocabularies of their parents when they were
children." Examples given in the pamphlet are *orbits, satel-
lites, detergent, bookmobile, tape recorder,* etc. Such words,
part of the huge jargon of gadgetry, can hardly be called
"new ideas."

The *Third's* approach to language ("Every person," said
Webster's promotional pamphlet, "is, in a sense, a dictionary"[23]) produced a dictionary devoted less to the art of
using words than to ideology. In the *American Scholar,*
Jacques Barzun, then dean of faculties and provost at Columbia University, called the *Third* "the longest political pamphlet ever put together by a party": "Its 2662 large pages
embody—and often preach by suggestion—a dogma that far
transcends the limits of lexicography. I have called it a political dogma because it makes assumptions about the people
and because it implies a particular view of social intercourse.
This is indeed why any page of the work provokes immediate
resistance or assent."[24]

Many defenders of the *Third* did not like Dean Barzun's
analysis (it quickly became famous), and they attacked him
with vigor. In *College English* Professor W. Nelson Francis,
chairman of the NCTE's Commission on the English Language, called a passage from Barzun's essay "either vicious
misrepresentation or arrant nonsense." Francis's subsequent
remarks on the nature of authority in language study reveal
that he wished the premises of the new grammar to obtain in
any discussion of the *Third:* "My point is that the public discussion [of the *Third*] has been carried out on grounds irrelevant to the discipline of linguistics and in ways that specialists in that discipline could not effectively counter because
the arguments brought up were not linguistic arguments at

all. Linguists like [James] Sledd and [Karl] Dykema who brought the illumination of their discipline and scholarly knowledge to bear on the controversy found themselves frustrated by the unwillingness of their opponents to meet them on the cold and clean plateau of rationality where scholarly argument and discussion rightly take place."[25]

On this "cold and clean plateau of rationality," Jacques Barzun had been called by linguist James Sledd an "intellectual bookburner" and the "corrupter of the American Scholar."[26] In a short passage of three sentences, linguist Karl Dykema by paraphrase and omission so seriously distorted Barzun's introductory remarks that Barzun was made to appear dishonest in his attack on the dictionary.[27] In another professional journal, Professor Kenneth Wilson had this to say about Barzun's article: "Dean Barzun's attack finally isn't just another ignorant and prejudiced review of Webster III, although it is both of those things: it is rather the hysterical outcry of a patriotic man, resentful of change and of the passing of time, and certain that all whose views of the world differ from his own are subversive; they are relativists who would pervert sound doctrine and right values, and therefore they must be stamped out quickly. In fact, it is a kind of linguistic John Birchism—pitiable and amusing at first, then disgusting, and finally dangerous in its childishly oversimple view of the world."[28]

The glare of publicity thrown on the new grammarians by the controversy over Webster's Third made them very uncomfortable. It was one thing to be controverted in scholarly argument but another to be ridiculed in the pages of the New York Times and the New Yorker.* What was worse, the

---

* Dwight Macdonald wrote a long, detailed essay on the Third in the New Yorker. Among other matters, he commented on the Third's labeling of enthuse and its citations: "Enthuse is labelled colloq. in Webster's Second but not in the Third. It still sounds colloq. if not godawf. to me, nor am I impressed by the Third's citations, from writers named L. G. Pine and Lawrence Constable and from a trade paper called Fashion Accessories."

new grammar, when tried in the schools, failed miserably. (We discuss that debacle in the next chapter.) With popular opinion adverse and support waning in the scholarly world, the new grammarians, although they continued to teach in the schools and universities, in a few years dropped out of public view. Toward the end of the sixties, the number of scholarly papers supporting their position had dwindled almost to nothing, and the NCTE had decided to pretend that the whole affair with *Webster's Third* had not happened. By a pleasant irony the *Third,* despite the negative reviews and curses heaped upon it, became an economic success; it sold more than 500,000 copies from 1961 to 1973.[29] This was probably the result of an innocent desire for guidance, not of approval of doctrine on the part of the buyers, who ordinarily do not study a dictionary or read its prefatory matter. The editorial practice of the *Third* has not changed; but the publishers did learn from history, and on issues grammatical grew quiet as a mouse.

While the idea of a "new grammar" was being abandoned, the permissive ideal in professorial bosoms burned stronger than ever, as did the desire for change. The new grammarians—now without any special identifying name or label—were joined by thousands of academic intellectuals bent on changing the schools and universities. In the late sixties, an unmistakable educational revolution occurred. In 1969, one of us was on a panel at a national meeting of English professors led by a man who had belonged to the new-grammar party. He came out strongly in favor of what came to be known as the "new English." We must, he said, "free up our English courses," by which he meant abolish the courses that covered writers before 1900, encourage elective programs, and remove the old-style composition course, with its "restrictive" requirements in theme writing. When one of the panelists disagreed with him, the leader turned on him in a vehement personal attack. The new grammarian was

with us again, seeking the familiar goal—an educational uto-
pia. Somewhere there must be the perfect ("new") English
course that would do for the student what school, church,
parents, and American culture could not do—make him literate, happy, and liberated.

A main constituent of the new English was the new rhetoric, a slippery subject. *Rhetoric* in this context refers to the
teaching of composition, grammar, and usage to college students. By the late sixties the chore had become unbearable
to all parties. Something had to be done. The advice from
the new English camp was mixed: (*a*) drop the course entirely; (*b*) make it a literature course with writing added; (*c*)
liberalize it by letting instructors and students design it
"creatively" at their own sweet will; or (*d*) do some, none, or
all of the above. A few very good institutions followed course
(*a*) on the grounds that their freshmen were "too well
trained" to take so basic a course. Other colleges, good and
bad, tried (*b*) and were for a time fairly satisfied. Many
places, including our own University of Illinois, tried various
combinations that led to spasms of student creativity everywhere, along with confusion and not a little angry criticism
from administrators, parents, and some legislators. Even one
governor's office took part in a wrangle over blue films being
shown to Illinois students in a course labeled Film as Rhetoric.

For seven or eight years, we kept a list of the contents
covered in the rhetoric course of typical American colleges
and universities. Picking from that list at random, one finds
business letters; personal diaries; short stories and poems by
students; modern literature of different kinds; the making of
collages, phonograph records, and home movies; western
novels; "great tragedies"; pornography; the history of the
subjection of women; the civil rights movement; rhetorical
models and techniques; argumentation; black literature; In-

dian literature; the facts of rape and its victims; haiku; personal essays; satires; stylistics.

At first glance no principle seems to govern the choice of topics or materials. But on reflection, a few antiprinciples emerge. Both teachers and students tended to avoid the standard fare of English and American literature—Shakespeare, Donne, Dickens, Hawthorne, James, Melville. They also avoided the study of literary history or criticism. Instructors often taught their own ideologies or intellectual hobbies. They generally ignored the substance of the old standard rhetoric or composition course—grammar, sentence structure, proper word choice, paragraphing, exposition, argument, and research technique. Writing was presumably taught apropos of any course content, from bridge building to transcendental meditation. In effect, those appointed to teach appeared to favor any device that did not involve teaching students to write.

Such schemes could not and did not work. They led straight to the uproar over the inept writing of college students and ultimately to a renewed concern about the rhetoric or composition course. From Berkeley to Cambridge, colleges and universities scrambled this way and that to right the ship. It was "back to basics," and on campuses across the land was heard the sound of students scratching out weekly themes. The press soon discovered the new trend; witness the widely read *Newsweek* cover story for December 8, 1975—"Why Johnny Can't Write." Our university, having tried everything it could think of, reestablished the standard composition course. Those instructors who had elected to teach movies or media ecology (be it noted that there is a professor of media ecology at one eastern university) have either found their way out of the English department or redeveloped their talents while also trying to look innocent.

When, in the competition of the intellectual market place,

117

a bad idea gets pushed aside, it does not necessarily go off in a corner and die. In the early 1970's, the notion of linguistic permissiveness lost favor for a time under the assault of the Back to Basics movement but soon returned at the call of a new slogan: The Students' Right to Their Own Language. In 1974, a constituent organization of the NCTE adopted this resolution:

> We affirm the students' right to their own patterns and varieties of language—the dialects of their nurture or whatever dialects in which they find their own identity and style. Language scholars long ago denied that the myth of a standard American dialect has any validity. The claim that any one dialect is unacceptable amounts to an attempt of one social group to exert its dominance over another. Such a claim leads to false advice for speakers and writers, and immoral advice for humans. A nation proud of its diverse heritage and its cultural and racial variety will preserve its heritage of dialects. We affirm strongly that teachers must have the experiences and training that will enable them to respect diversity and uphold the right of students to their own language.[30]

While asserting that the "standard American dialect" is a "myth," the committee of scholars making this statement uses that very dialect to write it. While encouraging "diversity" and denying the right of "one social group to exert its dominance over another," it employs thirty-two pages of explanation and bibliographic material after the resolution in its attempt to exert dominance over the linguistic training of children. And the committee sees no irony in its use of both Standard English and scholarly procedure to support the argument that knowledge of these should be denied to its own students. While being tolerant of what most people in the real world would call poor English, the committee's scholars do not write poor English. One wonders why they do not preach what they practice.

The cult of the antisnob snob evidently demands that while he writes clear, correct, idiomatic English, he must preach reverence for poverty-stricken usage. A sort of linguistic class struggle must be fought, which then becomes an emotional necessity. Thus, on page ten of the interminable tract called *Students' Right to Their Own Language:* "Many handbooks still appeal to social-class etiquette and cultural stasis rather than to the dynamic and creative mechanisms which are a part of our language." Such phrasing is weighted with political implications; note the setting of "social-class etiquette" against "dynamic and creative mechanisms." Indeed, as we move through the 1970's, the latest bad ideas about language still tend to be politics in disguise, and the confusion of professional and political matters by the NCTE has become commonplace. At its annual business meeting in 1976, the council decided to support the development of alternatives to standardized testing, while voting "to eliminate discrimination against gay men and lesbians" and passing a resolution against racism and "sexism."[31] And here is the council itself reporting on the editor of *College English* at the 1975 national convention:

> [The editor] forecast that "an industrial society will continue to want from us—or someone else—composition, verbal manners, discipline in problem solving, and docile rationality." He predicted that "liberal American capitalism will not really regain its balance, that those who control it will take sterner measures to keep their power, and that the choice will become sharper between a fascism that is their last resort, and socialism. The hope is," he concluded, "that what we do with the English curriculum will be done with that choice in mind and not from blind professional interest."[32]

American school teachers do not, as a rule, approve of the propagandistic nature of statements issued by the NCTE.

On our five-month tour of American high schools described earlier, we were at first amazed at the hostility expressed by representative English teachers toward their own organization—until it became clear that they did not consider it theirs. They had no voice in the running of the firm. They called the NCTE "political," "selfish," "unprofessional," "unrealistic." One teacher said, "The Council is living years behind the times, still back in the days of the Berkeley student revolt. It is run by idealistic professors who teach fifteen students a week, while we teach one hundred and fifty, and they make twice the money we do."

For years the general staff of the NCTE has been out of touch with the practicing teacher. Perhaps this is why the Council was caught so badly off balance by the Back to Basics movement, which was generally considered an attack on the new English. The movement became prominent before the Council had time to formulate a statement on the issue. So it reverted to the big-gun theory: at every opportunity, without reference to coherent premises, blast away against teaching the basics in English.

An example from the new deputy executive secretary of the council in 1976: "The public has an extremely shabby image of what's basic in the teaching of English. . . . we do know that formal teaching of grammar does not improve composition."[33] The president of the council in 1975 attacked the basics in that year's national convention, referring to "simplistic solutions." (Without the crutch of that phrase no NCTE executive could carry on his good work.) "Responding to 'Back to the Basics!' " he continued, "we often retreat to the worst basics from our worst seasons—to the rote drills and busy-work exercises that produce sterile environments and hostility from our students."[34]

When the National Assessment of Educational Progress issued its report *Writing Mechanics (1969–1974)*, which concluded that the writing of thirteen-year-olds and seventeen-year-olds had gotten worse, the chairman of NCTE's Conference on College Composition and Communication and the chairman of the NCTE Committee on Composition remarked in their joint commentary that "there is no evidence here that the schools must 'go back to basics'; indeed, the basics seem to be well in hand."[35]

It is clear that anyone who defends the idea of fundamentals in English has a hard time getting a hearing in the NCTE's publications. With a few exceptions, only the antibasics scholars may occupy the space in the national and state NCTE journals. The writer of the lead article in *College English* for January 1977 confides with characteristic charm that he is in favor of "reading and writing," which "are the essential things, the basics—not spelling, punctuation, grammar, and all that jazz."[36] The writer does not explain how to write competently without some understanding of all that jazz. Another well-known leader in the profession used an NCTE journal to say, "In the name of basic skills and basic literacy, we see a revival of methods and routines that the profession abandoned because they DID NOT WORK—because they were, for many or most of our students, wrongly based, counter-productive, pervasively negative in their whole orientation." This gentleman went on to recommend "full justice to the imaginative, creative, human dimension of language."[37]

Where, you might ask, in this debate concerning the basics, are the old-style professors and scholars, the ones we recall teaching Shakespeare, Dryden, and Chaucer to generations of undergraduates? Most of the regular English faculty in American universities prefer to take no part in either the controversy or the teaching of basic grammar and composition. When, in 1975, it was suggested at the University of Texas that members of the regular faculty might be required to teach one composition course (at any level) every third semester, the professors sprang to protect themselves from contamination. One remarked that the requirement might be injurious to "the recruitment of senior scholars for whom we compete with other schools. . . ." Another complained that freshman rhetoric "involves an overwhelming amount of dull, tedious drudgery" and that marking freshman essays "is a time-consuming, boring, uninspiring chore. . . ."[38] (We are happy to report that our own department recently voted to make freshman composition teaching a regular part of every English professor's assignment.)

An outsider might wonder why it is any less boring to mark twenty-five papers on James Joyce written by barely literate English majors than it is to correct the rather more varied themes written by twenty-five freshmen who—if they are typical of our freshman students—are somewhat better writers than English majors. It is ironical that English majors generally use the language worse than the better students in other fields. The reason? One college dean has ventured the guess that the less able students go into English because it is so easy.

Senior professors of English have seen to it that in most universities the teaching of composition and standard grammar is for slave labor only. Thirty years ago, we were both taught college composition by permanent, tenured faculty members. Now we would be taught by inexperienced teaching assistants, whose main interest usually is in literature and their own work for the Ph.D. Indeed, graduate programs are generally maintained by English departments so that senior professors can continue to teach seminars in modern Irish poetry, the Romantic period, or whatever, and have the use of their graduate students to teach freshman composition.

A young academic who even thought aloud about specializing in composition at any level would very likely meet his doom—that is, denial of tenure, assuming he could get hired in the first place. When asked about the possibility of hiring composition professors, the department chairman at Texas said, honestly enough, "In theory we would like to be able to do that, but it would be a disaster to those we recruited."[39] When Arn was interviewed years ago by a chairman at a major university, he was told, "I don't have a job for you; I just wanted to see the man with a Ph.D. who is crazy enough to put in writing that he wants to teach composition." From 1964 to 1966, five men and one woman—four with a Ph.D. and two who later got it—were hired to work in the composition program at a great state university. By 1970, three had become discouraged and left; two (excellent people) had been fired; and one was reluctantly kept by the department, which made it clear that there was no "real" place for a composition specialist in the English department. As we write this, the chairman of the freshman composition program at that university is an untenured assistant professor, who will not be allowed to stay.

Perhaps the classic professorial attitude toward the teaching of writing skills in college is implied in the title of the lead article in the profession's major journal, *College English*, for October 1976. The title reads "Freshman Comp: What is this Shit?" This might be called the excremental, rather than incremental, theory of English teaching.

The effects of such an attitude on those who go to teach in the public schools are predictably bad. Take a real case, that of Julie. Ten years ago, Julie was eighteen; she had attended an academic high school in a wealthy suburb. She had no grammar in high school, where she studied modern literature and creative writing and worked on the school paper. As a freshman at the university, she tested high enough on the machine-graded entrance exams to be put in a one-semester "advanced" class in rhetoric taught by a teaching assistant who himself had never had a college course in composition. Here Julie studied modern literature and wrote three papers, none of which was corrected for errors. She majored in English, most of her courses being in modern American literature, none directly teaching her the standard skills in composition. Upon graduation, she got a job teaching five classes of English (two of composition) in a middle-class high school.

At twenty-one Julie, the high school teacher, could not write an organized paragraph. The English sentence was a mystery to her, as were the techniques of fitting one sentence to another. She could not punctuate: "At college I just put commas where I felt they ought to go. Say, are there any rules for the semicolon?" She could not explain the sentence structure of most sentences; she could not teach students how to use certain forms of syntax properly, because she did not know what they were; she could not tell a main clause from a subordinate clause. She had no vocabulary to teach grammar with: "I teach sentences by the way they sound to me." Julie could speak fairly good English, although her vocabulary was limited and her ideas childish. But she could not write even passable prose, partly because she had not been taught to and partly because she had been filled full of bad ideas about language by her high school and college teachers.

No wonder illiteracy is catching. One can pass it around in society like a virus. Julie was a carrier and disseminator. From her, students caught the malignant sentence fragment, the chronic incoherency, and the incurable dangling modifier. But where did she catch these things? From her high school teachers, who caught them from professors in summer school and English Institutes sponsored by the federal government, the same who taught Julie and infected her. Her first teaching job lasted one year. The students diagnosed her weakness and devoured her alive. She became a secretary and over a period of years painfully learned the English language out of a secretary's handbook. Such is the cycle of incompetence in the teaching of English. From the bad ideas about language and composition to the students who become teachers and send more students back to the university, the whole wretched make-believe passes through the sphere of influence of the professor of English. Ultimately, the professor is responsible; or at least he bears a major share of the responsibility.

5.
Penetrating the Mystery
of Grammar

When the history of twentieth-century English is written, it may well be said of Americans that nothing in our language gave us more trouble than its grammar. Generally speaking, we do not teach it successfully to our children; our own understanding of it is fragmentary and sometimes flatly wrong. Most Americans arrive at middle age believing that grammar is as hard as differential calculus. If you look at the various theories of grammar put forth, you may well believe that it is harder than a dozen theologians could make it. From almost any angle, it is a most mysterious subject, particularly for those millions of people who have any interest, personal or otherwise, in the future of American schooling.

The great cynic Ambrose Bierce remarked that grammar was "a system of pitfalls thoughtfully prepared for the feet of the self-made man, along the path by which he advances to distinction."[1] With the wit removed, this is still the public's notion of grammar. For that matter, many teachers probably have about the same attitude toward the subject—grammar as a discipline related to propriety and socioeconomic advancement.

While there is no question that bad grammar holds many people back from activities in which their other talents might shine, the main issue regarding the teaching of the subject is at once broader and more fundamental. Teachers have no choice but to deal with questions of propriety like the use of *ain't* and the double negative. But they should concentrate more than they now do on the problem of what might be called attractive efficiency. Much writing fails because it is both inefficient and ugly, as in *Control of personnel is a necessity in maintaining computer room safety.*

Even when this sentence was put in its own context, a group of intelligent readers generally failed to understand the idea that the writer was trying to convey. By changing much of the grammar (and the wording), one can increase comprehension greatly: *To keep your computer room safe, ask all employees to sign in and out.* It seems futile, by the way, to argue which has the most influence in such rewriting—changes in grammar or in word choice. The fact is that in most sentences grammar and wording are so interrelated that changes in one affect the other. At any rate, the grammatical skeleton of the original is changed considerably in the revision:

ORIGINAL: Noun   *is*   noun

REVISION: Opener
                   [subject understood]   *action verb*   object

The question we have before us now is, How do we teach our children to write sentences that are both efficient and attractive? The old answer to the question was to instruct them in avoiding errors: the so-called negative approach. Like many old answers, this one has been tested by time and has much value in it. There is, however, something to be said for certain "positive" approaches to grammar that supply models for the young writer to imitate and practice on.

Before outlining a few positive grammatical methods, we should attempt to explain why grammar teaching of the recent past has had such small success. Consider, for instance, the record of transformational grammar in the schools.

In the 1960's, the transformational was the most popular of the new grammars written by academic professionals, largely because it did seem to lead to improved theories of language. Yet successful textbooks for most students were not forthcoming, largely because transformationalism is a theorist's grammar. We recently talked to a book salesman for one of the major publishers that sell high school grammars. "Transformational grammar is absolutely dead in the high schools," he said. "We can't even get teachers to consider a book with that kind of grammar in it."

The main reason for the failure of this grammar in the schools probably lies in its complexity. It is so difficult that neither teachers nor students can understand the rules of the system. One of the authors who tried to adapt the theory to school use by writing a grammar was Paul Roberts. Below is a part of his explanation of the passive construction, from *Roberts' English Series: A Linguistic Program* (1967). According to the publisher's promotional material, Roberts's textbook is meant for ninth-graders.

The passive transformation applies only to kernel sentences which contain a transitive verb and its object. In this transformation, the object becomes subject and **be** and the participle morpheme are inserted before the verb. The subject optionally appears at the end after the preposition **by**:

Ronald signed the contract. $\Rightarrow$

The contract was signed by Ronald.

What is the subject of the kernel sentence? What is the object? What is the transitive verb?

We can state the rule in this way:

$$NP_1 + Aux + V_T + NP_2 \Rightarrow$$
$$NP_2 + Aux + be + part. + V_T + (by + NP_1)$$

The numerals 1 and 2 under the NP's simply identify the noun phrases and show what becomes of them in the transform. What is the function of the **NP_1** in the kernel? What is the function of the **NP_2**? What does **V_T** stand for? What do the parentheses around **by + NP_1** mean? Apart from **by**, what morphemes occur in the transform that do not occur in the kernel?

Here is a fairly simple example of a sentence structure that might be transformed by this rule:

$$\underline{John} + \underline{past} + \underline{watch} + \underline{Bill}$$

<u>John</u> is the NP_1 of this structure. What is the NP_2? What is the V_T? What is the **Aux**?

Applying the passive rule, we first write the NP_2:

<u>Bill</u>

Then **Aux**:

<u>Bill</u> + <u>past</u>

Then **be + part.**:

<u>Bill</u> + <u>past</u> + <u>be</u> + <u>part.</u>

Then V_T:

<u>Bill</u> + <u>past</u> + <u>be</u> + <u>part.</u> + <u>watch</u>

Finally, if we like, **by** + NP_1:

<u>Bill</u> + <u>past</u> + <u>be</u> + <u>part.</u> + <u>watch</u> + <u>by</u> + <u>John</u>

Applying the affix transformation, we get this:

<u>Bill</u> + <u>be</u> + <u>past</u> + <u>watch</u> + <u>part.</u> + <u>by</u> + <u>John</u>

<u>Be</u> and <u>part.</u>, which were added together, are now separated. The insertion of word boundary will give us the T-terminal string:

\# <u>Bill</u> \# <u>be</u> + <u>past</u> \# <u>watch</u> + <u>part.</u> \# <u>by</u> \# <u>John</u> \#

Does a traditional book do the job of explaining the passive much better? Let us look at a famous modern text published within two years of *Roberts*—John Warriner and Francis Griffith's *English Grammar and Composition* (1969).

A verb is in the *active* voice when it expresses an action performed *by* its subject. A verb is in the *passive* voice when it expresses an action performed *upon* its subject or when the subject is the result of the action.

ACTIVE
VOICE   Lightning struck the barn. [subject acting]

PASSIVE
VOICE   The barn was struck by lightning. [subject acted upon]

All transitive verbs (those that take objects) can be used in the passive voice. Instead of the usual case in which the verb expresses an action performed by the subject and affecting the object, a passive construction has the subject receiving the action. Compare the following sentences.

                                        S   V   O

ACTIVE VOICE   On the third strike the catcher dropped the ball.

                                          S   V

PASSIVE VOICE   On the third strike the ball was dropped by the catcher.

                                          S   V

On the third strike the ball was dropped.

As you can see, to form the passive construction, the object of the active sentence is moved ahead of the verb and becomes the subject. A form of *be* is added to the verb, and the subject of the active sentence is either expressed in a prepositional phrase or dropped.

Notice that in the passive voice the main verb is always a past participle and that the tense is expressed by an appropriate form of *be*.

ACTIVE   Experienced pilots **fly** these planes.
PASSIVE   These planes **are flown** by experienced pilots.

ACTIVE   The sexton usually **rang** the church bell.
PASSIVE   The church bell **was** usually **rung** by the sexton.

The Retained Object

Active sentences that have direct objects often have indirect objects as well. When they do, either the direct or indirect object can become the subject in a passive construction:

                          S   V   IO   O

ACTIVE   The manager gave them free tickets.

                          S   V

PASSIVE   They were given free **tickets** (by the manager).

                          S   V

PASSIVE   Free tickets were given **them** (by the manager).

In both of the passive sentences above, one of the objects has been made the subject and the other continues to function as a complement of the verb. In the first sentence the direct object is retained as a complement; in the second it is the indirect object that is retained. The object that continues to function as a complement in a passive construction is called a *retained object.*

For anyone who tries to understand why grammar is so hard to teach, the partial failure of both *Roberts* and *Warriner* is instructive. Both texts give too much theoretical information. Roberts drowns the student in it. Warriner could cut his exposition at least by half. Grammarians often bewilder students and make teaching difficult because they want to "tell all." Even in relatively simple textbooks, they will try to tell us everything they know—and they know (or say) too much for good pedagogy.

Almost anything can be taught with some success, and grammar is no exception. Why then have the schools been failing? A look at Roberts's and Warriner's discussions of the passive provides one clue. Another is provided by considering the difficulties the "new math" encountered. Like the new grammar, the new math was a complex affair created by, and for, scholarly theorists. As early as 1962, Professor Max Beberman, one of the major figures in the development of the new math, raised serious objections to it: "I think in some cases we have tried to answer questions that children never raise and to resolve doubts they never had, but in effect we have answered our own questions and resolved our own doubts as adults and teachers, but these were not the doubts and questions of the children." Two years later, he commented that "we're in danger of raising a generation of kids who can't do computational arithmetic."[2]

In both the new math and the new grammar, the innovators had little experience of teaching people who were not theorists like themselves, who had in fact no need of theory but a great need of practical skill. The new grammarians did not live or work in the school world and had small interest in its problems. In their school texts, they tried to teach "morphemic analysis" (study of forms) or to put rigor in geometry at a time when many flesh-and-blood students could not add and subtract accurately, write intelligible sentences, or read well enough to fill out job application forms.

Now to pause for a look at some of the complexities of the subject that we easily and casually call grammar.

Professional grammarians tend to look at the subject from their own particular angles, according to the school of thought they belong to. Each school has developed its own premises and manner of analysis. The traditionalist, influenced by historical studies, uses a parts-of-speech approach that depends heavily on meaning and syntax. The structuralist, influenced by the social sciences, prefers to work inductively, devoting much of his attention to the forms and sounds of words. The transformationalist centers his attention on sentence making, supplying rules for the creation of "transformed" sentences from basic, or "kernel," sentences, which he assumes are present in the speaker's mind.

Each of these descriptions we are giving is oversimplified, yet each tells us something about modern academic grammarians who are, generally speaking, philosophical animals. They are not especially interested in showing the tenth-grader how to avoid making errors in his theme due next Tuesday. Instead, they are system builders, who spend their valuable time explaining to each other why one system applies to a construction and another does not. Theirs is an intellectual game, and to the winner goes the satisfaction of proving to other academicians that his system has fewer logical holes than the others have.

Grammar, to millions of Americans in school and out, is a very different affair. It is whether or not you use contractions, split an infinitive, use *hopefully* as a floating adverb, speak in a particular dialect, or write sentences that are acceptable. Grammar is that textbook stuff about nouns, verb forms, and *who* versus *whom* that one did not quite learn in high school, junior high school, or at mother's knee. Middle-aged executives have paid an editor well to read their manuscripts and "fix the bad grammar." They were on top of everything about their subject except that. Women, by the way, usually do better than men in practical grammar, a fact that may explain why schoolboys sometimes get the impression that it is a faintly lavender subject. But the great grammatical theorists, from Leonard Bloomfield to Noam Chomsky, to consider only the moderns, are all men. Let somebody else account for the fact.

If anyone thinks that most of us Americans—public school teachers, students, professors of grammar, textbook writers, members of the general public, and parents—are confused about what grammar is, he is right. For we all look at grammar from the standpoint of our need for it or difficulty with it. The professor wants to set up a flawless linguistic philosophy that will stand for a thousand years. At the same time, he has students to teach and dissertations to read: most of the important academic grammarians are graduate-school professors.

Parents have the problem of Junior, who has contracted something worse than the German measles, the symptoms of which are dozens of red marks on his school papers. This disease, members of the general public say, is never cured in school but is passed on to them in the form of illiterate business letters and unreadable scientific communications. Professors of grammar have the problem of instructing would-be teachers to teach grammar; but the latter universally maintain that they never really learned the subject "until we had to teach it to students." The textbook writer's problem is that he is blamed by all sides because nobody likes the way he interprets grammatical theory to the teacher, who must interpret it to the student, who "can't no way" explain it to his parents.

The interpretation of grammar is difficult because to study it is to study ourselves. With only slight exaggeration, it can be said that the study of language in its variety is no less difficult than the study of man in his complexity. Quickly as one gets a grip on one part of language, that part dissolves and becomes something else. "There is no *there* there," said Gertrude Stein of a place (no doubt in America) that she did not care for. In this brief sentence, the familiar English adverb *there* appears only as the last word. The first *there*, grammatically speaking, is not a word at all but a nullity. The second *there*—looking somewhat embarrassed—is temporarily serving as a noun.

Caution is to be exercised. Deliver yourself of a commonplace about English, even one that is old and respected, and be ready for the workings of our tongue to contradict you. Consider Charlton Laird, one of the ablest of modern linguists, who remarked in a textbook that "the expletive construction is essentially weak." Expletives are found in familiar statements like Gertrude Stein's. They begin with a *there* or *it* that has a grammatical function but no meaning, as in "*There* is a hint of spring in the air" or "*It* was wise to do those jobs." Professor Laird tested his premise on Hemingway, stating that one could read *To Have and Have Not* "for pages without encountering a single expletive. When I did find one, it was usually in a sentence that Hemingway seems to have deliberately made flat. . . . usually Hemingway makes his sentences work hard, and accordingly he avoids expletives."[3]

Yet if Laird had happened to pick up Hemingway's *A Farewell to Arms* and started to read at the beginning, he would have found in the first two pages ten expletive constructions, among them "There were pebbles and boulders" and "There was fighting in the mountains."

Then there is—block that expletive—the tired old grammatical saw about forms of *be: was, is, are, were,* might *be, been,* etc. *Be* is supposed to be the dullest and least colorful verb in English, invariably evidence of a comatose style. It is odd that William Shakespeare did not know this:

> To *be,* or not to *be:* that *is* the question:
> Whether 'tis nobler in the mind to suffer. . . .

Of course, not having had the benefit of a modern education, he did not know that a cloud hung over the expletive either:

> *There* are more things in heaven and earth, Horatio,
> Than are dreamt of in your philosophy.

Turn at random to almost any famous passage from this greatest of writers and you will find English grammar mined for whatever grammatical ore it will yield, regardless of the presence of our hated *be*'s. For instance, Prospero's beautiful speech in *The Tempest:*

> Our revels now *are* ended. These our actors,
> As I foretold you, *were* all spirits, and
> *Are* melted into air, into thin air.
> . . . .
> We *are* such stuff
> As dreams *are* made on, and our little life
> *Is* rounded with a sleep.

Here, Shakespeare uses *be* verbs either as linking devices or as a part of the passive construction. It is true that bad writers overuse *be* forms; but then bad writers are capable of misusing any forms in English, including the most vibrant of active verbs.

Caution, we say, is to be exercised regarding every aspect of English and its grammar. (This includes admonitions against the passive voice, which we have used to start two recent paragraphs.) The situation in every aspect of language is wonderfully complex. Let us listen to a first-rate modern linguist, Dwight Bolinger, describe it:

> It is evident . . . that our mental computers are constantly at work storing the expressions that we use according to certain internally elaborated regulations, endeavoring to bring order into an otherwise chaotic un-system of individual words and phrases, putting each where it can be found when needed. The linguist ferrets out the formulas and states them as grammatical rules, but ordinary speakers create them. Variations in amounts of data and sharpness of contrast explain why at the core of its grammar a language is almost immovably regular, but at the edges it defies rigid formulation and mocks all rules with hosts of exceptions—and also why, if a language could be subjected to an overall system such as Esperanto or Basic English, it would still go spiraling off sooner or later like a disobedient cloud of gas from a central sun.[4]

It seems likely that a good share of the grammar children study in textbooks belongs not to the core but to the edges of English. That may explain why "textbook grammar" (the grammar of the educated) is so hard for many people to learn: "it defies rigid formulation and mocks all rules with hosts of exceptions." We seldom teach core grammar in the schools because we already know it from childhood.

We have speculated enough. Now down to earth and a specific case. Consider this simple sentence, an example that we borrowed from a textbook: *The wind blew out the candle yesterday.* After inspecting this sentence, and remembering what we know about other typical sentences in English, we can make observations like the following: (*a*) *The* must come before *wind; wind the* makes no sense. The same is true of *the candle.* (*b*) *Blew* indicates a time relation; other forms of the verb (like *will blow* or *was blown*) indicate a different time relation. (*c*) *Out* can be considered a little piece of the verb, as if the whole verb meaning *extinguished* were written as one word: *blewout.* (*d*) *Yesterday* belongs to a class of words that tell us when, where, how or to what extent. Words in this class, called *adverbs,* often appear with an *-ly* on the end: *clearly, sweetly, hungrily.* But *slovenly* and *likely,* in ordinary idiom, do not belong to this class of words. (*e*) *Yesterday* can be moved to other places in the sentence: *Yesterday* the wind . . . or The wind *yesterday.* . . . But not *The yesterday wind blew out.* . . . (e. e. cummings might write this in a poem, but most of us would never think of saying or writing it.) (*f*) A special relation exists in the statement made, a relation that can be symbolized like this:

Subject	Transitive verb	Object
wind	*blew out*	*candle*

Transitive, from the Latin for "passing over," is a grammatical term that helps to describe statements of this kind, in which the "movement" of the meaning in the sentence seems to pass from the subject to the verb and then to the object. Millions of sentences like this are possible in English.

Other observations could be made about the sentence.[5] For example, the subject *wind* of the verb is a naming word, and it is in a typical subject position, toward the front of the sentence. Using the same words that we already have, we could rewrite the sentence thus: *The candle blew out the wind yesterday.* This is perfectly grammatical, although it is not logical.

What observations can be made about the sentence that would probably not be grammatical ones? It is not a grammatical observation to say that the sentence is true. Perhaps there was no wind yesterday and Susan blew out the candle. That fact does not touch grammar directly. It has nothing to do with grammar that the sentence is a line of blank verse: *The wind/blew out/ the can/dle yes/terday.* We cannot say that *yesterday* should be moved to a different place in the sentence or that the idea might be better (or worse) phrased in different words: *Four and twenty hours ago, a zephyr crushed out the life of the candle's flame.*

In short, grammar does not deal directly with truth (one can lie grammatically), beauty, effectiveness, diction, or rhetorical techniques in general. A statement can be dishonest, ineffective, ugly, stupidly worded, and a palpable horror but still be perfectly grammatical: *Media deception creates a viable necessity in this day and age for the maintenance of an operable relation vis-à-vis American non-allies.*

English grammar, then, deals mainly with the form and organization of the sentence and its parts. When you speak or write an English sentence, you put its parts together according to a code. If one reads the following statement fast, it may seem incoherent and totally ungrammatical, a complete violation of the code: *Persons shouldn't hug kiss when meeting a friendly handshake indeed as effective* (written by a college freshman). Yet by supplying two words and a pause marked by punctuation, we have an intelligible sentence: *Persons shouldn't hug and kiss when meeting. A friendly handshake is indeed as effective.* If the freshman had spoken his original statement instead of writing it, he would probably have inserted the words he needed. Like many people, he got grammatical lockjaw only when he sat down to write.

So much, quickly, for grammar at, or near, the core of language. The edges of language are covered by usage, which refers mainly to the disputed, or debatable, elements in English. They may involve matters of propriety, grammar, pronunciation, idiom, metaphor, or word choice. About the only parts of English they do not involve are those found in the hard core of the language—for example, certain patterns of word order (*the girl* instead of *girl the*) and subject-verb agreement (*we are* instead of *we is*). Yet even the second example can be considered a legitimate issue in usage, since *we is* has been both understandable and acceptable to certain members of the English-speaking population. Preferences concerning *we are* versus *we is* can be debated.

Many of the debatable points of usage are found in those linguistic edges where "good English" and "what people say" conflict. Is it *none is* or *none are? Different from* or *different than? To run madly* or *to madly run?* These, however, can be settled, according to the preferences of the debaters, by referring to one of the authorities on usage: H. W. Fowler, *Modern English Usage;* Bergen and Cornelia Evans, *A Dictionary of Contemporary American Usage;* Theodore M. Bernstein, *The Careful Writer;* and Wilson Follett, *Modern American Usage.* Often a good standard desk dictionary, such as the *American Heritage Dictionary of the English Language,* will help. Less easy to settle are those disputes over what might be called the social or ideological questions of usage regarding slang, euphemisms, fad words, obscenity, political jargon, and so on.

Children learn the core of the language early and quickly. When a two-year-old daughter says, "Me lubba you, Mommy," she is using core grammar and ignoring the edges, which she cannot manage yet. And she knows exactly how that remark differs from another piece of core grammar: "You lubba me, Mommy?" It will take her years to master the edges of English: the use of *like* as a conjunction (right or wrong?), whether to end a sentence with a preposition, how to distinguish *between* and *among.*

To teach grammar, one must know it, have some practical control of it and its basic terminology. How well are the students in teacher-training programs prepared to teach the subject? For years, Arn has been offering an undergraduate course in grammar for teachers. For the course Charlene provides material, criticism, and an occasional lecture. We do this in a university known for the high quality of its student body, in which, for example, half of the freshman class of 1975 was drawn from the top 10 percent of the high school classes and 84 percent from the top quarter. At the beginning of the course, which is designed for English majors who plan to teach, we have often given a little quiz on basic grammar. Results go something like this: out of a class of twenty-five, two can identify a subjunctive in a sentence; four can identify all the parts of speech in a simple sentence; four will understand what is meant by a split infinitive; three will know the distinction between a clause and a phrase; none can define the term *subordinating conjunction* accurately; none can identify subordinate clauses accurately; four will know what a dangling modifier is. Their fund of misinformation makes one have dark thoughts about their teachers' powers of literary observation: over twenty will believe that one should not start a sentence with *and* or *but* or end it with a preposition; that forms of the verb *be* should be replaced with "stronger" verbs; and that studying more of the same sort of grammar they have been mislearning for years will help them to be better writers and teachers. It might be mentioned that many of them are abominable writers.

These English majors are not stupid. They are pretty well motivated: they want to learn grammar if they can find out what it is and how to get on top of it. They hope to improve their writing and learn to teach children to write. They are vaguely aware that the grammar they learned—or did not learn—has been of little use in writing good themes and papers. What they need is instruction in how grammar and rhetoric support each other and how a knowledge of certain parts of grammar can lead to good writing.

For the very few Americans who are talented, writing is an art. For the rest of us, it is mainly a craft or skill. It can be learned in different degrees of excellence like any craft or skill—by firm instruction and diligent practice. Consider a promising young quarterback. He will practice hand-offs and pass patterns hour after hour until they become automatic. In a game, he makes his successful plays not by remembering letters and lines on a coach's blackboard but by trained instinct and developed reflexes. A young violinist improves his bowing technique by learning from an instructor the proper way to hold the bow, flex his wrist, and draw the bow across the string. He spends hours of practice on bowing and finger exercises.

This method of teaching and learning has significance. No coach of a junior team directs his youthful quarterback "to move his ulna with the flexors." Instead, he will say, "grip the ball like this and snap it forward quick—watch how I do it." The violin teacher does not speak of metacarpals, phalanges, and tendons but of holding the bow in a particular way and moving it "like this." Such teachers employ illustrations using the surface elements of the act and repeat the admonition to practice.

But when we teach grammar in relation to writing, we usually ignore the surface elements. Many teachers do not know what they are. They are not gerunds, participial phrases, predicates, and adverb clauses. As the medical terms of grammar, so to speak, these are hardly more useful to the child who writes than are *metacarpals* and *phalanges* to the same child whose ambition is to play the fiddle without squeaking. (At some point in his training the student can benefit from a careful introduction to grammatical terms. That point probably occurs after he has learned to write basic sentences quickly and easily. If he has had good training in the primary grades, he will find terms helpful in junior high school, at which time simple theory will reinforce his understanding of skills already acquired. If he does not have these skills by junior high school age, no amount of slogging through a typical grammar book is likely to help him much.) It is obvious that if one needs to create state-

141

ments that make sense, he will have to practice sense-making statements. He should practice a pattern until he can produce it quickly and with ease:

Pattern: Smiling, the boy fell dead.
Practice: Laughing, she left the tennis court.
Practice: Smiling at his joke, she walked on the court with her friends.
Practice: Sneering at his weak serve, she smashed it into the opposite court.
Practice: Yelling with outrage at the umpire's call, she stalked toward the net.

It is this pedagogical technique that the theoretical scholarly studies seldom take into account. They look for a correlation between the study of a philosophical system and the performance of a skill. It may be that a correlation exists, but the youngster learning to write will not perceive it and cannot make use of it. Nor will twenty-year-old English majors who are preparing to teach.

There are some difficulties with our argument, and they should be faced. First, the analogy between one kind of skill (playing football or the violin) and another kind (writing an English sentence) is possibly strained. Being different activities, they might well require different methods of teaching and learning. Also we may be begging the question in asserting that we should teach those parts of grammar that help the writer to create "sense-making statements." What are they? Furthermore, we pretend to teach the sentence without using terms like *gerund, adverb clause,* and *predicate*. Can a subject be taught without an array of technical terms?

The most formidable difficulty confronting the teacher of grammar is the ideology of modern teaching in America. For years teachers have been repeating that drills are unnecessary, boring, and Victorian; that imitation is bad because it is

not "creative"; that students should write their own sentences, not imitate others'; that not all students can learn to
write; that we should avoid setting up a system that has failure built into it.

Let us admit that there is some truth in each of these objections. But given the nature of human beings, and also the
nature of teaching and learning, one suspects that more
truth resides in the original formulation. If grammar is to be
taught, let us by all means teach it with vigor and require
that the student learn it with thoroughness. Here is a sketch
of how the job might be done.

In the early grades, students should practice writing short
sentences: *My cat is black. Melanie's father likes to drink
beer. The sun did not shine yesterday. I am happy because
it's Friday.* The teacher puts such typical sentences on the
board and asks students to imitate them using different ideas
and subjects. She asks for original sentences that the students make up. She checks the sentences for sense and correctness, setting up a proofreading system. Every day the
work must be properly done, proofread by the student, and
checked by the teacher. In addition to these exercises, the
teacher can add workbook drills in grammar—subject-verb
agreement, change in pronoun forms, and so on. But at this
point it is not necessary to use grammatical terms (*verb, pronoun, subject*). After all, the child has been using his language for a number of years; he learned to speak and communicate decently without ever knowing a verb from a
pronoun. What we are doing is continuing this natural learning process in a systematic way through imitation, correction, and, on the student's part, production of new sentences
that he makes up from his own experience of the world and
from reading.

The skills of using proper forms and making sentences can
be combined in the workbook:

Pick the correct word and put it in the space.

(a) Johnny gave it to _____.   (I, me)

(b) _____ and Barbara don't fight any more.   (she, her)

(c) The ball and bat _____ lost.   (is, are)

In the three spaces below, write new correct sentences like (a), (b), and (c) above.

(a) _____

(b) _____

(c) _____

The student is now gaining skill in making simple statements, building up his knowledge of form and structure, and gaining good habits in the use of English. All of this work is both oral and written, since good oral usage is in the real world often as important as good writing. Pronunciation must be clear, accurate, and reasonably standard. The teacher should correct all mistakes in writing and insist on clear handwriting, good spelling, and proper form generally. If students are allowed to be careless or lazy at this stage, they will develop bad habits that they may never overcome.

After the students have mastered the simple statement, the teacher can move on to the practice of compounding (but the word *compound* does not have to be used):

John and Alice are sick today.

I like *hamburgers and malts*.

The wind blew hard last night, but *the icicles on my house did not break*.

Students should practice using the comma before *but* (or *and* and *so*) in sentences like the last one.

So far, our teaching of punctuation has been restricted to end punctuation and the comma used in the compound before an *and, but,* or *so.* Next we introduce sentence bases and free units and the use of the comma and the semicolon:

I like hamburgers and malts, *although Mom says they aren't good for me.*
The wind blew hard; the icicles did not break.
By the end of the year, I'll need new shoes.
The woman next door, *who doesn't hear well,* never answers her doorbell.

In this simple, but very useful and flexible, system the student learns to handle what the teacher knows as certain types of phrases, main and subordinate clauses, subordinating conjunctions, and standard methods of punctuation. But the terminology is kept simple, as before. The *sentence base* (in Roman type in the examples above) is a complete statement of the kind that the student has had practice in writing. To this base he adds a *free unit* (the italicized words) and punctuates the "joint" between the base and the free unit. It does not matter whether the free unit is a clause or a phrase, since the technique of "addition" is the same:

The angry man +   , *yelling loudly,* + ran after me.
Beginning to yell loudly, + the angry man ran after me.
As he ran after me, + the angry man yelled loudly.

It is useful for the young writer to see definite patterns in sentence making. Nothing confuses or discourages him more than formless blobs of writing that he does not know how to imitate, much less discuss, using the terminology of traditional grammar. Before he came to school, he learned English by using his ears and mouth; now he will use his ears, mouth, eyes, and hands. The suggested patterns in the system are consistent; take a base and add a free unit to it:

When grandma visits, we have waffles every morning for breakfast.
Grandpa, *who still has all his own teeth,* would rather have bacon and eggs.

Punctuation is a part of the system, for it is done automatically at the joint where the free unit is added to the base. The student should read, write, speak, and listen to such sentences, using all his faculties to get a feel for the constructions. He needs to be able to write the major patterns without thinking, as automatically as he catches a baseball. So far as the terms of grammar are concerned, he needs only these: *base* and *free units*, these last being of three kinds, *openers, interrupters,* and *closers.* Unlike most grammatical terms, these mean just what they seem to mean. Bases are the main or complete statements, while free units are incomplete and are detachable from bases. As free units, openers, interrupters, and closers do what their names imply—open, interrupt, and close sentences. After a time, the student can solve workbook problems like these:

1. Fill in the blanks with *free units* or *bases:*
   (a) If _____, we'll never get to the movie.
   (b) Mrs. Markham's old tree, which _____, crashed into the top of their garage.
2. (a) Write a sentence using *while* at the beginning of an opener.
   (b) Write a sentence using *but* between two bases.
   (c) Write a sentence using *who* with an interrupter inside a base.

This system is adapted in part from the modern grammar developed by Francis Christensen, but it is much simpler than Christensen's.[6]

The program just described can start in the third or fourth grade and end with the sixth grade, the natural breaking point between grade school and junior high. Throughout this period, the teacher should emphasize all the skills of communication: reading, writing, speaking, and listening. He should train his students to read aloud, pronounce words properly, and listen for the rhythms of good prose. Students should often have an opportunity to speak carefully in the classroom and should have their more obvious mistakes corrected. It is at this age when the arts of imitation are most important, when good habits are acquired easily by youngsters imitating the work of older, more accomplished persons. No chance should be lost to show them how the good writer turns a phrase or how the good speaker emphasizes a word or makes his pronunciation distinct. Above all, this is the time for practice and drill. Youngsters at this age can take without serious complaint a considerable amount of drill and correction that they will balk at later. Moreover, if they learn the basic patterns of good speaking and writing early, they will not have to repeat the same work through junior high, high school, and on into college and graduate school. Few activities are more depressing to all concerned than "remedial" writing in college. The sight of brawny men and full-grown women painfully trudging their way through grade-school English—subject matter that they should have learned years earlier—is enough to make teachers weep and taxpayers vote down school bonds.

In junior high school, students can begin on a somewhat different program that for the first time will employ extensively certain elements and terms of traditional grammar. Up to this point, they have been building on their natural methods of acquiring language, which is mainly through the use of eye, ear, and voice and the constant practice of patterns, but without the injection of theory. Now they will learn about parts of speech, phrases, clauses, modification, and the like. But they should study only that material which bears upon writing and speaking correctly and accurately. Any part of grammatical theory that does not help them in some way to communicate better and to understand discussions of good work should be avoided if possible.

Which parts of traditional grammar ought to be stressed in junior high school? The study of English grammar is difficult because language consists of complex interweavings of meaning and structure. In many instances, it is impossible to disentangle meaning from structure, and vice versa. Furthermore, many operations in English are carried out as sets of more or less unique signals—idioms, for example, like *came thick and fast;* merged verbs, like *put up with* for *tolerate;* or semilogical rhetorical signals, like *at any rate,* placed at the beginning of a sentence.

The trick is not to lose oneself in a grammar that tries to explain everything and thus lose the student in a maze of details. Some grammatical "details" are more important and fundamental than others. Examples in some problematic areas are given below.

The Parts of Speech

In ordinary sentences, one can usually identify the jobs most words are performing. In our last sentence, for example:

prep.	adj.	noun	pron.	v.
In	*ordinary*	*sentences,*	*one*	*can*
adv.	v.	adj.	noun	adj.
usually	*identify*	*the*	*jobs*	*most*
noun	v.	v.		
words	*are*	*performing.*		

In this useful table of the parts of speech "interjections" are ignored:

The Part of Speech	Does Something
Noun ⎫	
Pronoun ⎭	names
Verb	states
Adjective ⎫	
Adverb ⎭	modifies
Preposition ⎫	
Conjunction ⎭	joins

Students will have trouble with joiners and with verbs acting as other parts of speech (verbals). As joiners, prepositions and conjunctions can be kept separate by noting that prepositions appear with nouns in this pattern: *in* the well, *over* the tree, *against* my will. The preposition-at-end (*That idea is the very one I am against*) tends to take care of itself. Verbals are probably best identified as "verbal nouns" or "verbal adjectives." Accordingly, verbs can be roughly divided into two classes: sentence verbs (The engine *was running*. The house *burned*. His will *should be done*.); and verbals—either verbal adjectives (the *running* cat, the *burned* house) or verbal nouns (*Jogging* is tiresome. That is what I call *cheating*. *To do* wrong is often fun.). Using this system, students can usually see the difference between sentence verbs and verbals:

v. adj.	v. adj.	sent. v.
The *burned* steak	*sizzling* on the stove	*should be thrown* away.

v. adj.	v. noun	sent. v.	v. noun
That *smiling* way of *deceiving*		*is*	what I call *cheating*.

This system makes no pretense to completeness. The idea is to give students enough terminology and basic knowledge of how words work so that they can benefit from observations on usage and rhetorical effectiveness. It is useless, for instance, to tell a student that many adverbs "float" and can be moved to various places in the sentence, if he does not know what an adverb is or that it is the most movable of the parts of speech. One needs to know basic grammar and some of its technical terms in order to discuss such questions of usage as *like* as a conjunction, as in *Do it like I do*. The fact that *like* can be verb, preposition, conjunction, noun, adjective, and "verbal idling" or mere noise, as in *I had, like, three dates last week,* strongly supports the premise of this rhetorical grammar: the parts of speech are named according to how they act in a particular sentence or construction. If a word acts like a naming word in one construction, it is a noun there. If it acts like a verb in another construction, it is a verb there. That idiom tends to influence how some words act as parts of speech is, of course, a relevant truth in improving the rhetoric of students. Also relevant is the ambiguity of many grammatical signals. The idea in the following sentence can be finished in two basic ways: *He does it better than (I [do]/ me)*. When the writer gets to *than,* its signal is so faint he does not know whether it is a preposition or a conjunction. (Usage remains divided on *than I* versus *than me.*) In the following sentence, *smiling* is grammatically ambiguous: *She had been smiling and happy all morning.* L. M. Myers, whose example this is, comments, "*Had been smiling* looks like a verb phrase. *Smiling and happy* looks like a pair of adjectives. Argument is useless—take your choice." [7] Argument may well be useless in such cases, but discussion for the young writer has some value because it can reveal important insights into his language.

The Phrase

Most grammars start with the part of speech and work their way up through larger units—from word to phrase, to clause, to full sentence. This is symmetrical theory but doubtful practice. For the very young writer in the lower grades, it is more natural to begin with what he is familiar with—the sentence that makes a statement. Later, he can learn the parts of speech and then go on to the clause, skipping the theory of phrases except for learning one point about them and one only. For hardly anything in the study of grammar gives students more trouble and less genuine help than identifying phrases by name. Consider these two sentences:

The large dog *barking on the lawn* belongs to my neighbor. *Hurt by the tone* of her angry voice, he picked up his books and left.

Most students will not understand why *barking on the lawn* and *hurt by the tone* are both participial, a term they find troublesome. And if phrases are supposed to be fundamental units, why aren't the phrases identified as *on the lawn* and *by the tone?*

After long experimentation with the classroom study of phrasal grammar, we have concluded that the whole business might as well be ignored. We teach two grammatical elements rather firmly, the part of speech and the clause. The phrase we define as any natural unit of words "larger" than a single word and smaller than a clause. The phrase has more than one word in it, but it cannot make a statement in the way a clause can. Typical phrases look like this:

> Jerry *had placed the water bucket* so that we *could not see* it *at the bottom of the well.*

Longer phrasal units are often made of smaller ones: *at the bottom of the well.*

Grammatically speaking, phrases tend to take care of themselves. One uses them when he needs to:

> The bucket was found at the bottom *of the well,* not *by the edge of the cistern.*

Considering phrases rhetorically, there are a few useful things that can be said about them. The main concern of the writer is to make them accurate and, secondarily, to keep them short. One should not pile them up:

> Look for the phonograph record of Mary's in the old album in the cardboard box by the staircase in the back of the house.

Piling can be reduced by rearranging phrases into smaller units:

> Look for Mary's phonograph record in the old album in the cardboard box, which is by the back staircase.

Individual phrases should be kept short (and logical):

> If we had kept strong, there *might not even have been* a threat of World War III today.

This becomes:

> If we had kept strong, there *might not be* a threat of World War III today.

The fact that phrases are small units probably accounts for their movability; they seem more flexible in this way than clauses. But they are also more susceptible to logical calamity:

(a) There are twenty-eight programs for the service man divided into two sections.

(b) With a comb in one hand and a toothbrush in the other, a thought struck me.

(c) Mr. Anderson said in his office there must be no carelessness.

(d) We reached the theater and seated ourselves three rows from the front upon his suggestion.

The issue in sentences like (a)–(d) is one of logic. The ideas in them do not connect properly, so the teacher's job is to show the student why they are illogical and how they can be rewritten to make sense. Sufficient practice over a period of time will drive the point home.

The Clause

A clause is created by marrying a noun and a verb.

BRIDGET *cursed.*
CATS *will meow.*

The APPLE and the ORANGE *might have been eaten* and *thrown* away.

Once joined, a noun subject and its verb belong together and are dependent upon each other. Modifiers and complements may be added in dizzying profusion, but the nature of the clause does not change—a noun with its own verb, a verb with its own noun.

The clause is the heart of grammar. In it one finds a place where grammar and rhetoric firmly support each other. It is true that single words and phrases can in certain sentences be all-important—for example, an opening *but,* a phrase of qualification, a descriptive adjective. Even a punctuation mark can assume great significance; lawsuits have been won and lost on commas. Yet it is only with the clause that we customarily make statements, complete or not:

(a) I *am.*

(b) HE *performed.*   SMITH *was.* . . .

(c) SANDRA *died.*   WHO *was.* . . .

(d) POLICY *is.* . .   WHAT THE POLICY IS *remains.* . . .

In ordinary sentences, clauses are usually filled out with modifiers and complements. Modifiers change or affect an idea somewhat; complements "complete" an idea already started on its way. Filling out the examples above, we might have:

(a) I *am* the master of my fate.   [main clause]

(b) Even though HE *performed* cruel acts, SMITH *was* not really a cruel man.
                    [subordinate and main clause]

(c) SANDRA, WHO *was* injured when the bridge fell, *died* a few hours later.
                    [subordinate clause inside main clause]

(d) WHAT THE POLICY IS *remains* a mystery.
                    [subordinate noun clause as subject
                    of main clause]

The theory of subordinate clauses need not be made difficult. So far as the young writer is concerned, they are formed exactly as are main clauses, by a noun married to its own verb; and subordinates use modifiers and complements in the same way that main clauses do. The differences between main and subordinate clauses are, first, that subordinate clauses are incomplete statements and, second, that in practice such clauses are generally "signaled" by one of a rather small group of words or phrases such as *which, since, if, while, what, so that, who, because, that, though, although,* and *where*. These *subordinating signs*, as they may be called, tell a reader that subordination is occurring. In (b)–(d) above, note *though* in (b); *who* in (c); and *what* in (d). Occasionally, subordinating signs can be omitted: *I know [that] he is guilty.*

Why is a knowledge of the clause so important for the young writer? Simply because to write sentences is to make statements, and the young writer ought to know how clausal statements are usually made and in what typical patterns. Some typical patterns, with the subordinating signs capitalized, follow:

(a) Main clause: *I won't eat lunch today.*

(b) Subordinate clause as opener: *SINCE my stomach hurts,* I won't eat lunch today.

(c) Subordinate clause as closer: I won't eat lunch today, *THOUGH the cafeteria is serving my favorite food.*

(d) Subordinate clause as interrupter: The cafeteria, *WHICH is serving my favorite food,* will probably ruin it.

(e) Subordinate clause as subject: *WHAT the cafeteria does to food* is unbelievable.

(f) Subordinate clause as object: I don't know *HOW they manage to ruin food so consistently.*

If the student has practiced the techniques we refer to as (1) "sentence base and free units" and (2) "clausal patterns," he will have a fairly complete view of how most ordinary sentences are made in English and how they are punctuated. The theory is relatively simple, and if he practices the patterns hard, he will increase his stock of options as a writer.

We cannot emphasize this last point too much. Teachers of English do not agree on a great deal, heaven knows, but most of them do agree that students at all levels have a dreadful time just writing consecutive logical sentences. This happens partly because their stock of sentence options is so small. One can read through dozens of ninth-grade compositions, for example, and never find a noun clause used as a subject. Most students are not aware that the pattern is available to them.

By way of concluding this section on grammatical fundamentals, let us repeat that teachers should avoid getting lost in detail. The list of terms should be kept short and basic. Moreover, they should avoid grammatical explanations that have no bearing on making a sentence effective and true. For instance, the grammar of adverb clauses is impossible to explain clearly to most students, and knowing about it does little for the writer. Yet for many years, textbook authors have taken it for granted that instruction on adverb clauses is necessary. Here are two examples, written nearly sixty years apart, of how adverb clauses are supposed to work:

(a)   *Although I do not like his manners,* I respect his character.

(Kittredge and Farley, *Advanced English Grammar,*
1913)

(b)   *Because two pictures were on the TV screen,* we could watch both the football game and the launch countdown.

(Hodges and Whitten, *Harbrace College Handbook,*
7th edition, 1972)

In neither case can students easily see why the subordinate clauses are "adverbial." The relation appears to be one of logic rather than of modification. And if the clauses are modifiers, why don't they modify the entire idea in the main clauses that follow? If we shift the opening clause in sentence (b) to the end of the sentence, it seems even less adverbial.

While on the subject of subordination, it might be mentioned that the elaborately inconsistent nomenclature for subordinating signs drives students crazy. In the sentence *When I see the man who found her, I'll be happy,* what is the point of calling *when* both an adverb and a subordinating conjunction or *who* a relative pronoun? "*Who* is 'relative' to what?" an exasperated college senior asked the other day.

By the end of their junior high school experience, students should have learned the positive facts about the sentence that we have outlined. We make little mention of what might be done with grammar in the tenth through twelfth grades. If the proper groundwork is laid, teachers in the later high school years may well work on writing problems as they arise. As much as he can, the teacher should continue to stress the sentence as the fundamental element of grammar, discussing the smaller elements such as the parts of speech when he needs to. The key is practice and discussion. Over and over students should write sentences, correct and proofread them, and discuss in class the results of their work. At the same time, the teacher can conduct necessary drills in structure and idiom. Of course, literary studies form a good basis for discussion of grammatical choices. Why did Mark Twain use this construction here? Why did Stephen Crane use a different one in a similar situation?

One positive fact about the sentence that we have found useful blends grammar and rhetoric. This fact is that the main clauses in most sentences fall into four classes of statement, as follows:

(1)	Action statements	(a)	The trailer swayed.
		(b)	Dad wrecked the trailer just now.
(2)	*Is* statements	(c)	The trailer is a mess.
		(d)	Mom will be mad.
		(e)	The man who got off his motorcycle might have been a cop.
(3)	Passive statements	(f)	The trailer will be replaced by Dad.
		(g)	The insurance had been paid.
(4)	*It/there* statements	(h)	There will never be another trailer like it.
		(i)	It's a bad day for the Smith family.

This classification of statements is controlled by the relation between the subject and verb of the main clause and by the type of verb employed. *Action* statements employ action verbs which may or may not have objects, as in (a) and (b). *Is* statements use any form of *be* or other linking verb such as *seem, appear, become. Passive* statements are made in the familiar way. *It/there* statements start with an expletive or filler phrase.

Grammarians have set up more complicated classifications of statements. In one of his textbooks, Paul Roberts counted out ten types, isolating constructions like *They made him king* and *They gave him a crown*. To simplify, we ignore such constructions—for that matter, they can be easily classified as action statements—and also ignore imperatives and questions. The latter two cause no trouble to speak of in students' writing.

Like the other aspects of "sentence grammar," the classification of statements is valuable because it shows the student that there is a relation between what he says and how he says it. If he wants to show an action, he may use an action statement. If he wants to show an equivalence (*My father was a Democrat*) or a quality (*Harold is good-tempered*), he may use an *is* statement. The passive statement is appropriate for variety or for ambiguous situations in which the agent is not known (*The bottle was thrown against the house*). It is also useful for emphasizing the subject of the sentence. The *it/there* statement is appropriate for beginnings. (*There were two major weaknesses in the defensive team last year*) and for conditions (*It's a beautiful day in San Francisco*).

Knowing and practicing the four statement types gives the writer a greater range of techniques in sentence making. We find that many students have been strongly warned away from passive, *it/there*, and *is* statements. "Use action verbs!" goes the pedagogical cliché. Yet if you pick up almost any extended piece of well-made prose, you will find the four statement types employed by the writer as he needs them. For instance, the passive allows the writer to place toward the end of his sentence a noun about which he wants to add description:

(*a*) The charge was leveled against the MAYOR, *who refused to comment until he had seen his lawyer.*

(*b*) The poor will not be helped by any TAX *that takes earning power from them.*

The *it/there* statement can make a beginning, state a condition or circumstance, give an opinion or judgment, or introduce facts. Example of the latter: *It's untrue that the mayor refused to comment.*

The *is* statement can express a quality, characteristic, or condition, as in these remarks on soap opera written by Stephen Koch:

But perhaps we should not altogether despise soap opera. It *is* the one really original narrative form thus far contributed to art by broadcasting, and one fine day it may even produce its masterpieces. Now, the secrets of soap opera *are* these: it must *be* about family life (threatened family life, motivated especially by sex, money, power, and challenged loyalty), and it must *be* endless. . . . In soap opera people do not come to conclusions. They react; visually, soap opera *is* the great art form of the reaction shot. And merely reacting, rather than concluding, the characters live their lives chewed up by time. A soap opera *is* not a narrative form defined by the beginning, middle, and end of an action or an event. On the contrary, its basic unit of imagined time *is* the span of the generations.[8]

The statement types we have been discussing belong to the grammatical core of the language and, as such, will not change in the foreseeable future. When the student learns to manage structures like these, he is taking an important step to controlling the language, which he often feels—with justifiable bitterness—is busily controlling him. Along with grammatical dexterity is developed rhetorical flexibility, as when a writer consciously uses a grammatical device for the sake of emphasis or rhythm. Indeed, our theme in this chapter is the value of conscious choice in managing the language: when a young writer constructs a sentence and knows how he is constructing it, he has attained a certain power over himself and his surroundings. And a certain power over his future.

6.☆
What to Do

There is a risk in trying to rescue American English from its difficulties. History is littered with the wreckage of schemes for the improvement of tongues. Human beings are, however, scheming animals; and we should perhaps follow our natural inclination to try to set things right, even in matters linguistic. Yet we might keep an eye on the past and avoid those utopian attempts to halt the decay of tongues, reminding ourselves that we are not so much picking the best method—if there is a "best"—but one that avoids the errors of the worst. Let us follow the principle inherent in the third element of Kittredge's new "grammatical category" of comparison, which he is said to have discovered—so the Harvard tale runs—while listening to two townsmen discussing the virtues of a dog. Said one man, "He's a damned good dog! He's a God-damned good dog! But I don't know he's such a hell of a God-damned good dog."[1] One can't go far wrong following that line of skepticism.

We divide our suggestions for improvement by addressing different groups of Americans.

What Citizens Can Do

Attack bad uses of the language whenever and wherever possible. Do not let letters written in jargon or gibberish leave your office or home. Let your local schools know that you will test for ability in English every graduate you interview for any job. Why should you hire illiterates? If you cannot understand a communication or if it is badly written, send it back to the writer for an explanation. Do not be afraid to criticize. Refuse to buy or subscribe to magazines and newspapers that publish pretentious, pedantic, or smart-aleck prose. Write to editors when you are especially aroused by nonsense. Here is a model written two hundred years ago by the Secretary to the Commissioners of Excise to the Supervisor of Pontefract: "The Commissioners on perusal of your Diary observe that you make use of many affected phrases and incongruous words, such as 'illegal procedure,' 'harmony,' etc., all of which you use in a sense that the words do not bear. I am ordered to acquaint you that if you hereafter continue that affected and schoolboy way of writing, and to murder the language in such a manner, you will be discharged for a fool."[2]

Do not assume that it is your fault if you cannot understand a piece of writing. Most subjects, except for those requiring truly technical language, can be explained so that they can be understood. Most people who write unintelligibly want to make their subject more mysterious than it is in order to feel important and superior or to deceive the public in some way. Turn the tables on them. A Houston principal wrote a message to parents that included this sentence: "Our school's cross-graded, multiethnic, individualized learning program is designed to enhance the concept of an open-ended learning program with emphasis on a continuum of multiethnic, academically enriched learning using the identified intellectually gifted child as the agent or director of his own learning." One parent wrote the principal: "I have a college degree, speak two foreign languages and four Indian dialects, have been to a number of county fairs and three goat ropings, but I haven't the faintest idea as to what the hell you are talking about. Do you?"[3]

Look into your local schools. What are they doing to improve the use of English? Find out about those who are running for the school board. How do they feel about the teaching of English? Consider helping someone start a private school in your community. A major weakness of the American educational system is that the public schools have almost no competition.

What Parents Can Do

Support your child's teacher in her efforts to teach composition. It is one of the most difficult jobs a teacher works at because it requires her to deal with experiences close to the student—his idea of how something happened, what it is, or how it ought to be. Teaching composition also calls for a great deal of advance preparation on the part of teacher and students, and yet more time from the teacher for correcting papers.

For grade school: Check your child's homework, particularly his writing assignments. Observe the kind of writing he is expected to do. If he writes nothing but poetry, sketches, and short stories, ask the teacher why expository writing is not assigned. In so-called "creative writing," much bad work can be excused because—in the typical remark made by students—"It's just the way I feel, and you've no right to tamper with my feelings." Study the paragraphs your child writes. See if they hang together and follow from a clear topic sentence. Does your child seem to have a fair command of vocabulary? Can he write in complete sentences? If not, see what the teacher is doing to help him understand sentence making. Make sure that your child is getting instruction in all of the basics: reading, writing, grammar, usage, pronunciation, spelling. Study his textbooks and talk to the teacher.

For junior high and high school: Continue checking on the matters mentioned above. Make sure that your child is getting at regular intervals—preferably at least every two weeks—a writing assignment that is carefully graded and returned to him. Even if the teacher has a load of one hundred and fifty students, that is still only seventy-five papers a week, which ordinarily is not an excessive demand on the teacher's time. Look at the grades and comments. Is the teacher perhaps teaching your child to write badly? Does the teacher mark errors in punctuation, spelling, and grammar? In logic, word choice, and content? Does it appear that the students have had suitable preparation before starting to write? If not, perhaps you should have a conference with the teacher. Preparation is all-important.

Expect all your children's teachers to correct papers for grammar, spelling, punctuation, logic, and content, not just their English teachers. If teachers of science, social studies, or home economics are ignoring illiterate nonsense, then go to the teacher and ask why.

Never take no for an answer. Look into everything. Every once in a while, go to the school and walk around in the building. Talk to the administrators. If you do not get satisfaction, go up the line as far as necessary. Complain. Organize. It is your child and your schools. They are taking your tax money; get something for it in return.

For college or university: Call on the administrators of the English department. Find out how the writing courses are staffed. All of the instructors teaching advanced writing should be full-time professionals, and at least half of those teaching the freshman course in composition should be also. All teaching assistants should have supervisors who watch over their classroom work and paper grading. Look into the exemption policies of the freshmen course; if more than about 10 percent of freshmen are exempted from the course, it is likely that the institution is trying to save money by not teaching some of its best students to write. Since World War II, universities and colleges have starved freshman English programs; an English department may hire a professor in

Renaissance literature at $35,000 a year while refusing to keep an experienced composition teacher making $10,000. An important administrator in our university recently told one of us that there is "plenty of money" for new or experimental programs in composition, but none for tried ones. In other words, money is available for pedagogical stuff and nonsense.

Find out how many papers are required in the freshman writing course. If a student does not write at least twelve corrected papers in a semester, he is not getting sufficient practice. What are the paper-grading policies? Are they clearly stated? What is the grading curve? Is there a syllabus? Take it away with you and read it. If the institution to which your community sends its young men and women does not have a good program in composition, find out why and ask for changes.

What Public School Teachers Can Do

Join the NCTE and get involved in your state affiliate. Persuade your affiliate and the national NCTE to take a stand against bad or unrealistic pedagogical theory and practice. Do not be intimidated by those college professors who are contemptuous of the classroom teacher. Tell them that they may be out of touch with school facts and functions and, if necessary, that they do not know what they are talking about. Do not allow the theorists of the profession to dictate classroom activities that are clearly unworkable.

Teach a practical, not a theoretical, grammar. Do not teach grammar as a subject in itself, but for the sake of improving composition. Do not be afraid to be inventive in applying grammar to the writing required in your classes. Make each writing assignment worth the student's effort. Prepare the class in advance of writing assignments, discussing possible thesis statements, varieties of theme organizations, and strategies for attacking the subject. An assignment to "write a paper on *To Kill a Mockingbird* for tomorrow" is useless without preparation. If you have no training in teaching composition, read some of the books and journal articles on the subject.

Even if your teaching load in composition is heavy, do not give up. Use the class period for theme conferences; allow students to read and evaluate others' writing. Discuss common errors with the class whenever possible. Demand more practical textbooks that tie grammar instruction to actual writing. If possible, do not use textbooks that teach grammar in the abstract.

What School Administrators Can Do

Keep the teaching load of English teachers to one hundred twenty-five students or fewer.

If you have an elective system, require at least one term of composition, grammar, and usage every year. Abolish silly electives.

Demand that composition be taught in all English courses.

Delegate authority to a superior teacher and leader to act as department chairman of the English department. Release her from one class for each ten teachers in the department. Make her responsible for curriculum and in-service training.

Help this chairman to develop a strong in-service training program for teaching grammar, usage, and composition.

What Students Can Do

Do the assignment! Writing is hard work, but it is like any other skill: practice leads to improvement. If a teacher gives you a poor grade or writes critical comments on your paper, it does not mean that your teacher dislikes you. Your paper is not you. Remember from one paper to the next the critical comments on your work so that you will not make the same mistakes over and over. Also consolidate the gains you make on each paper so that you continue to improve. If there are corrections or comments that you do not understand, ask for an appointment with your teacher to see how you can improve. Make the corrections, based on the comments of the teacher. Before writing a paper, plan carefully; no one can write a first draft without an outline or plan. Much of the hard work of writing is in the planning. Then revise your first draft, more than once if you can.

Watch how good writers—those you like to read—use the language. Pay attention when you read, and try to imitate writers you respect and enjoy.

What English Professors Can Do

In your department, treat the problems of teaching composition as being equal to those of teaching literature. Encourage graduate students who have rhetoric appointments to take the teaching of composition seriously as a useful part of their graduate work. Do not tell graduate students to give their composition teaching short shrift in order to spend more time on graduate work in literature. Discourage graduate students from turning their composition courses into literature classes.

Be a teacher of writing. Expect good writing from both undergraduate and graduate students. Since many of them later will be teaching composition, show them how it can be done. Offer to teach a class of composition yourself.

In your teacher-training courses, do not treat all methods of teaching composition as equally valid or useful. Make some decisions about the most useful methods, based on your own experience. See that undergraduate students in teacher education have an opportunity to evaluate student writing, and work with them before they have their student-teaching assignments. Encourage students to take a professional, businesslike attitude toward teaching composition and grading papers.

All these suggestions are common sense, but they lack an informing principle. For where schooling is concerned, all of us—parents, teachers, students, taxpayers—manifestly lack a sense of purpose and organization. America is, however, a nation of joiners. For improving the language, and our use of it, we propose creating an organization for civilized Americans who would prefer a civilized tongue. This might be called the American Society for Good English. *Good* means the opposite of *bad*—at least when it does not mean something else.

The purpose of the Society would be to make English more precise for reading, writing, and speaking. If it could help to make English easier and more agreeable to read, more beautiful, few would object. Members of the Society would be drawn from all walks of life, but especially from professions whose practitioners use the language and have a stake in its being used well: journalists, engineers, scientists, lawyers, editors, manufacturers, union members, professional writers. We exempt professors from membership unless they individually admit and repent past errors. Let us have from them no more cant on the value of "creative writing" or the unscientific "scientific grammars." Away with the elaborate formulas for analyzing foggy styles and the smart slogans of semantics—"The map is not the territory".

What should the American Society for Good English do? A model for some of its activities can be found in the *Prospectus* of the Society for Pure English founded in England in 1913. An important passage of the *Prospectus* reads as follows:

> The promoters of this association (which calls itself the 'Society for Pure English') are of course well aware of the danger of affectation, which constitutes the chief objection to any conscious reform of language. They are fully on their guard against this; and they think that the scheme of activity

which they propose must prevent their being suspected of foolish interference with living developments.

The ideal of their proposed association is both conservative and democratic. It would aim at preserving all the richness of differentiation in our vocabulary, its nice grammatical usages, its traditional idioms, and the music of its inherited pronunciation: it would oppose whatever is slipshod and careless, and all blurring of hard-won distinctions, but it would no less oppose the tyranny of schoolmasters and grammarians, both in their pedantic conservatism, and in their ignorant enforcing of new-fangled 'rules,' based not on principle, but merely on what has come to be considered 'correct' usage. The ideal of the Society is that our language in its future development should be controlled by the forces and processes which have formed it in the past; that it should keep its English character, and that the new elements added to it should be in harmony with the old; for by this means our growing knowledge would be more widely spread, and the whole nation brought into closer touch with the national medium of expression.

The Society, therefore, will place itself in opposition to certain tendencies of modern taste; which taste it hopes gradually to modify and improve.[4]

In another place, the *Prospectus* states:

Now, believing that language is or should be democratic both in character and origin, and that its best word-makers are the uneducated, and not the educated classes, we would prefer vivid popular terms to the artificial creations of scientists.[5]

If we were living in the world of 1913 and were proposing to establish our American society, we might borrow all of these principles from the English group. But in the 1970's the corruption of the "uneducated" by a dozen forces in our culture requires us to be skeptical of their ability as word makers, and the decay of standards of speech and writing among the educated in this country may cause us to be a trifle more authoritarian in matters of usage. Specifically, the American Society for Good English should be hard on garblers and jargoneers who alike use vague or fad expressions—Unspeech. This vagueness may come from choosing an empty word like *prioritize,* a nonspecific word like *concept,* or a weapon word, as in "male *chauvinist.*" In certain contexts these words might find a conceivable use, but generally they lack precision and often, especially the weapon words, are question-begging. Propriety, in questions of usage, must take second place and precision first. An occasional exception to this rule is the four-letter obscenity, whose usefulness in invective and love-making has been vitiated by overuse in speech and print. Now become lamentably weak, the obscenities will have entirely lost their force when they appear, as they may before long, in cigarette advertisements: "PUFFS taste real f***ing good, like a cigarette should."

Many of the original members of the Society for Pure English were scholars, and their tracts were as a rule scholarly and theoretical. The new American organization should not oppose theoretical endeavors, but its main purpose should be to note and discuss the good and bad uses of English in the special context of American life. A monthly journal of comment would be instructive. Problems of syntax, style, diction, and logic need rigorous analysis; but the quasi-grammatical pseudo-issues of the split infinitive, preposition at end of sentence, double negative, use of *ain't* and the *who-whom* snare are best left to Professor Grumble. The danger to English today, as Jacques Barzun has written, "is not from bad grammar, dialect, vulgar forms, or native crudity, but from misused ornaments three syllables long. The enemy is not illiteracy but incomplete literacy. . . ."[6]

Moreover, let the society set down its opinions, prescribe vigorously, and freely use the words *good, bad, better, best.* Writing a clear sentence requires the art of a craftsman: it may also be a moral act. One must condemn as bad the pompous stupidities of the educationist and sociologist. Much of the word fog produced in political writing and speaking is simply evil, the "defense of the indefensible," George Orwell called it in "Politics and the English Language":

> Defenceless villages are bombarded from the air, the inhabitants driven out into the countryside, the cattle machine-gunned, the huts set on fire with incendiary bullets: this is called *pacification*. Millions of peasants are robbed of their farms and sent trudging along the roads with no more than they can carry: this is called *transfer of population* or *rectification of frontiers*. People are imprisoned for years without trial, or shot in the back of the neck or sent to die of scurvy in Arctic lumber camps: this is called *elimination of unreliable elements*.[7]

Orwell's examples are dated, but his principle applies to the language of this morning's newspaper.

The reader will note that we have omitted mention of certain small practical matters—how the Society can be financed, its meetings arranged, its publications written, and so on. If the right men and women join and run it, these things will doubtless take care of themselves. But neither government nor the universities should be allowed to get their hands on it, appoint committees, and ask such questions as "What are the psychological components of oral language?" The Society would then become just another monster created by the cohabitation of education and government.

A second proposal that should be considered springs from the belief that anyone wishing to improve the use of English requires a standard to look to—or to ignore, if he likes. We therefore propose that the American Society's first duty would be to make authoritative statements on the English curriculum at all levels. Such a curriculum for high school, along with suggestions for reading and writing, could give teachers, parents, and school boards an idea of how their school might improve its work. Call the curriculum anything you like—the American Standard, perhaps. Schools could offer the Standard as their option parallel to existing programs so that eventually its efficacy could be judged competitively by those close to it. If the Standard proved useful, students would voluntarily enroll in it, teachers ask to teach it, and universities single it out as a requisite for enrollment.

Now for objections to all these suggestions and proposals.

It can be objected that societies for improving language have been tried before and failed. So they have. In the long run, most of the projects we human beings try will fail. Shall we then give up?

It can be objected that schools should not have a curriculum imposed upon them. No imposition is suggested. Schools can take the American Standard or leave it.

It can be objected that the American Standard does not take dialects and the linguistic problems of minorities into account. Anyone making this objection should consider the success of Harlem's P.S. 192 in teaching reading. In 1968 this school exceeded the national averages in reading on the Metropolitan Achievement Test, doing significantly better than similar schools. How did this happen? The principal simply said: We are going to teach reading; we will expect teachers to teach and students to learn. At the time, the native language of about half the students in P.S. 192 was Spanish. The teachers started out in Spanish, then moved to English. As the Council for Basic Education reported, "Throughout the school, Spanish is treated with respect as an important language in today's world. (In contrast, the school makes no concessions to what has been called by some 'the inner-city English dialect.' Dr. Seymour Gang [the principal] says that the school does not worry about it, uses standard English. He comments characteristically that 'the dialect problem' is important only in the educational and sociological literature.)"[8]

The black psychologist Kenneth Clark said in an interview, "The educational establishment, it seems to me, is content to continue to discuss interminably the problems of the 'disadvantaged.' It is willing to consider theory after theory, but seems very reluctant to act." We have permitted the discussion on teaching and learning, Clark went on, "to be dominated by an unprecedented amount of theory and abstraction, in psychiatry, psychology, and sociology, when it's basically a pedagogical problem." The issue is effective teaching. "I do not know of a single situation," said Clark, "in which minority group children have been taught efficiently, effectively, and with compassion and understanding and skill, in which their performance has not been at or close to the norm of the performance of other children equally well taught."[9]

It can be objected that the American Society for Good English with its suggested curriculum would be—we blush to use the word—moralizing. It certainly would be. But no matter how Pecksniffian we waxed, we could never purvey the moral line like our American ancestors, to many of whom good grammar was more than just avoidance of error. According to some Victorians, if one used the language correctly, linguistic uprightness seeped over into the other compartments of one's life and produced a fearful goodness in every cranny. Here, over a century ago, is the grammarian Samuel Kirkham addressing the "Young Learner": "Nothing will be more effectual in enabling you to think, as well as to speak and write, correctly, than the study of English grammar, according to the method of pursuing it as prescribed in the following pages. . . . Remember that 'knowledge is power;' that an enlightened and a virtuous people can never be enslaved; and that, on the intelligence of our youth, rest the future liberty, the prosperity, the happiness, the grandeur, and the glory of our beloved country."[10] Judged by that standard, our moralizing will be weak and pale indeed.

It can be objected that the members of our American Society, being drawn from the ranks of the successful users, rather than theorists, of the language, will lack authority, and that they will oversimplify linguistic issues. Such complaints have been used in the recent past by pundits and promoters of the new grammar. Two examples: (*a*) "As we proceed, we hope it will become increasingly obvious that the study of language, like language itself, has order, discipline, and system, and that consequently the layman's opinions about language are no more reliable than his opinions about medicine, physics, or engineering."[11] (*b*) "People who talk about 'correct English' are usually oversimplifying the problem dangerously. There IS no single, monolithic 'correct English.' "[12] The logic is a bit strained. English is not a discipline like medicine, physics, or engineering. Most American "laymen" never study medicine, but most of them study English. Millions use the language daily, some of them with grace and precision.

It helps also to state a linguistic problem with an eye on the real world. Who was it, do you suppose, who told the author of (*b*) that correct English was *single?* Have you lately heard even a whisper of the proposition that "correct English is monolithic?"

Many of the best authorities on matters of everyday usage are educated men who live and work outside the schools and universities. The *American Heritage Dictionary of the English Language* sensibly included on its usage panel persons such as Theodore Sorenson, lawyer and special counsel to President Kennedy; Red Smith, sports columnist; Katherine Anne Porter, novelist; John Kieran, writer and naturalist; Hodding Carter, newspaper editor and publisher; George

Gamow, physicist; Alistair Cooke, social historian. The schoolmen on the panel—such as Jacques Barzun, Donald Davidson, and Gilbert Highet—were in the main well known as writers and were anything but cloistered academics.

It will be objected that the American Society for Good English is going to be filled with snobs, elitists, and purists. In one weekend's reading in the professional literature this year, we encountered the word *purist* twenty-eight times. It is a catch-all curse, designed to bring anyone who questions the ideology of the new grammar or new English to his knees. It is used in the most Orwellian manner possible.

The "purist" has become the Emmanuel Goldstein of American English. Goldstein is the "Enemy of the People," the object of the Two-Minutes' Hate in George Orwell's *1984*. Goldstein, like the purist, is "the primal traitor. . . . All subsequent crimes against the Party, all treacheries, acts of sabotage, heresies, deviations, sprang directly out of his teaching. Somewhere or other he was still alive and hatching his conspiracies. . . ."[13]

Like Goldstein, the purist is never seen. His very existence is in doubt, but he must be reinvented and regularly denounced in the strongest terms possible. He is the straw man of the new English, always described as believing in a cold and formal correctness that does not deviate from Standard English. He is socially rigid and reactionary and accepts no dialects but his own. He is turned into a plural and called hard names: "the language purists, the legendary fussy Miss Thistlebottoms," in the phrase of one new-Englisher. Does one detect a little sexism? Why *Miss* Thistlebottom?

But the purist is worse than just fussy, as a professor of linguistics at Cornell has informed us:

> Aside from mere ignorance of the facts, there are only three psychological bases for purism: sadism, masochism, and de-

sire for personal aggrandizement. Authoritarianism in any field (including language matters) is based primarily on sadism, the desire to force one's will on others and to cause unhappiness while doing so; most purists are, consciously or unconsciously, sadists. Some people do get pleasure out of masochistically yielding to the will of others and obeying puristic precepts. Most contemptible of all are those who adopt puristic attitudes because they find that, by truckling to prevailing superstitions, they can obtain *kudos* from that part of the public who know no better (incidentally fattening their bank accounts in the process).[14]

Well, well, now we know.

As for the ever-ready charge of snobbery, what is a snob? The *American Heritage Dictionary* says, "1. An arrogant or affected person who strives to flatter, imitate, or associate with people of higher station or prestige. 2. One who despises his inferiors and whose condescension arises from class or intellectual pretension."

In modern America, as compared with Europe, what might be called standard snobbery is rare. Our tendency toward classlessness provides little encouragement for it. Who is above an American that he might wish to flatter or imitate? Whom can he find to despise? We have worked with both laboring men and college-educated professionals. We do not recall anyone in either group yearning after the life of a class above him or bothering—through "intellectual pretension"—to call an inferior despicable. The truck driver and the chemist may want more money, a better house, a bigger car, a new rug on the living room or office floor. They can express strong aversion to Poles, blacks, or the "white trash" who just moved in down the street. But what they ordinarily strive for is not class-oriented status but particularities: a new television with a bigger screen or the feeling of security that might be gained by driving a rough-acting family from the neighborhood.

Snobbery in America is not so important a problem as antisnobbery, which has become part of the intellectual's political religion. It begins, as V. S. Naipaul remarks, "by sympathizing with the oppressed and ends by exalting their values."[15] In the reasoning of the intellectual, down is up, so far as usage is concerned. He feels sorry for the black at the bottom of the ladder and hastens to adopt his dialect—or part of it. How astonishing during the civil rights crusade a few years ago to hear murmurs of "Right on!" in a faculty meeting of white English professors.

In the logic of the antisnob snob, impoverished usage is sacrosanct. "Students have a right to their own language," the NCTE believes officially. The National Association for the Advancement of Colored People (NAACP) feels differently about the issue, apparently less concerned with cant about snobbery and democracy than with teaching black children to read and write. In objecting to a course in black English being taught at Brooklyn College in 1971, the NAACP editorially remarked in its magazine, *The Crisis*, that black English was a "cruel hoax": "What our children need . . . is training in basic English which today is as near an international language as any in the world. To attempt to lock them into a provincial patois is to limit their opportunities in the world at large. . . . Let our children have the opportunity, and be encouraged, to learn the language which will best enable them to comprehend modern science and technology, equip them to communicate intelligently with other English-speaking peoples of all races, and to share in the exercise of national power."[16]

What holds for black children holds for white, Indian, Mexican, and Oriental children—for all American children of whatever background. To condemn inaccurate, slovenly, or unmusical usage is not the act of a snob. More likely, it is the act of someone who cares about both the language and the human beings who speak it.

It can be objected that we should not disturb the natural development of English. The process of history is the proper corrective. The new grammarians have always taken it as an article of faith that living languages are constantly changing and today's errors are absorbed into good speech: wait until tomorrow. On this basis, the best solution is to do nothing. Let history take its course, without interference. Over time the common man can be trusted to rid the language of its pedantries and preciosities. No less a sage than Ralph Waldo Emerson taught us to respect the lingo of the common man. "The language of the street," he wrote, "is always strong. What can describe the folly and emptiness of scolding like the word *jawing?* I feel too the force of the double negative, though clean contrary to our grammar rules. And I confess to some pleasure from the stinging rhetoric of a rattling oath in the mouth of truckmen and teamsters. How laconic and brisk it is by the side of a page of the *North American Review.*"[17]

But in America the common man, who actually may have had some of the linguistic virtues attributed to him, is rapidly disappearing. Emerson's truckmen are now cabdrivers who study law in night school and want their sons to go to Harvard. The teamsters of our era live in suburbs, serve on school boards, and talk of "concomitant learnings" and "custodial assistants" just as though (like the school superintendent) they had two degrees from Columbia Teachers College.*

The processes of contemporary history are working not for the language but against it. Owing to complex social changes, we have in our population fewer and fewer "assured speakers" of any social group. Given a press (here

* The common man of any time loves verbal nonsense. One remembers the story of the parish-beadle (as related by F. L. Lucas in his *Style*) who was asked how he liked a sermon: "I watna, sir, it was rather o'er-plain and simple for me. I like thae sermons bae that joombles the joodgment and confounds the sense."

including radio and television) that reaches almost everywhere in the country with extraordinary immediacy, we are influenced in our diction and our thought less by the daily events of necessary labor than by the jargon of a dozen trades and professions.

If you are middle-aged, you remember as we do the silences of our youth. Long, long periods of quiet. In school, utter silence in the study halls. Silences at night after supper. When company came, reading in bed in an adjacent room. Newspapers, books, magazines read in silence. With fewer distractions, we paid more attention to what we read—which perhaps explains why most literary materials in the thirties and forties (even the pulp fiction) were written in prose that today seems almost too careful in grammar and syntax.

We could hope for a return to the silences of the past and to better edited prose to read. But in the meantime, we are being linguistically Balkanized, as Wilbur Samuel Howell wrote in an essay discussing modern rhetoric. He said that "unless our learned men can be taught to speak to each other and to the people, we shall create on the one hand a set of Balkanized knowledges and on the other a schism between the people and the intellectual classes. That sort of schism will make the demagogue our master, even as a Balkanized learning will destroy the unity of our culture and the meaning of our spiritual life."[18]

It is toward reunifying ourselves and our language that we should work, starting today. Our premises are that some excellent questions about language have no answers, or at best partial ones, and that there are clear truths and fuzzy ones. As Aristotle remarked, "precision is not to be sought for alike in all discussions. . . . it is the mark of an educated man to look for precision in each class of things just so far as the nature of the subject admits; it is evidently equally foolish to accept probable reasoning from a mathematician and to demand from a rhetorician scientific proofs."[19] Nor must we take ourselves too seriously.˙ As G. K. Chesterton said, "When a man begins to think that the grass will not grow at night unless he lies awake to watch it, he generally ends either in an asylum or on the throne of an Emperor."[20]

Above all, avoid the snare of the intellectual—utopianism. The human animal is not to be made perfect, nor are his works. The goal is not to be perfect users of English but better ones than we now are. In all its aspects—grammar, idiom, logic, usage, rhetoric—language is inseparable from morality. The right and wrong of a practice cannot be discussed unless we use words. And we cannot begin to understand the complexities of moral questions until we use words accurately and employ the appropriate grammatical adhesive to bind them together. What Watergate showed, among other things, is that a failure in the proper use of English can be a failure in both thought and morality.

A more serious result of the American abuse of English is deeply personal. As our public rhetoric becomes more churlish and illogical; as our plays, movies, and works of fiction become more slovenly, violent, and dirty; as our scholarship becomes more pretentious and inaccurate, so our American spirit loses its magnanimity and grows weak and mean-spirited. To abuse language is to abuse the very idea of being human. Wit, kindness, intelligence, grace, humor, love, honor—all require the right employment of language for their embodiment. In the decline of American English may be also seen the decline of the American as human being.

References

Chapter One

1. Willard Thorp, "The Well of English, Now Defiled, or Why Johnny Can't Write," *Princeton Alumni Weekly* 59 (1958): 6.
2. Richard Poirer, "The War Against the Young." *Atlantic Monthly*, October 1968, p. 55.
3. Albert Marckwardt, *Linguistics and the Teaching of English* (Bloomington, Indiana: Indiana University Press, 1966), pp. 133, 74.
4. Barron Beshoar, *Hippocrates in a Red Vest: The Biography of a Frontier Doctor* (Palo Alto: American West Publishing Co., 1973), p. 83.
5. *Ibid.*, p. 227.
6. George Orwell, "Politics and The English Language," *The Collected Essays, Journalism, and Letters of George Orwell*, eds. Sonia Orwell and Ian Angus (New York: Harcourt, Brace and World, 1968), 4: 130.
7. George Plimpton, ed., "Katherine Anne Porter," in *Writers at Work: The Paris Review Interviews*, 2d ser. (New York: Viking Press, 1963), p. 157.
8. Hortense Calisher, "The Guest Word," *New York Times Book Review*, September 22, 1974, p. 47.
9. Patrick Ryan, "Your Happy Taxonomist Uses 39 Words to Say 'Dog,' " *Smithsonian*, March 1972, p. 84.

10. Douglas Bush, *Engaged and Disengaged* (Cambridge: Harvard University Press, 1966), p. 246.
11. Stanislav Andreski, *Social Sciences as Sorcery* (New York: St. Martin's Press, 1972), p. 61.
12. Hao Wang, "On Formalization," in *Contemporary Readings in Logical Theory*, eds. Irving Copi and James Gould (New York: Macmillan, 1967), pp. 36–37.
13. Alan Smith's remarks are reprinted in Alan Smith, *Science*, June 10, 1977, p. 1182.
14. Francis Straus, letter to *Science*, September 29, 1972, p. 1154.
15. Bruce Price, "An Inquiry into Modifier Noun Proliferation," *Book World*, April 12, 1970, p. 8.
16. Dwight Bolinger, "Truth Is a Linguistic Question," *Language and Public Policy*, ed. Hugh Rank (Urbana, Illinois: National Council of Teachers of English, 1974), pp. 168–169.
17. Chief Justice Warren dissenting, Shapiro v. Thompson (1969).
18. United Press International story, dated November 10, 1976.
19. James J. Kilpatrick, *Chicago Daily News,* July 8, 1976.
20. Evelyn Waugh, "An Open Letter to Nancy Mitford," *Noblesse Oblige*, ed. Nancy Mitford (New York: Harper, 1956), p. 112.
21. D. H. Naftulin, M.D.; J. E. Ware, Jr.; and F. A. Donnelly, "The Doctor Fox Lecture: A Paradigm of Educational Seduction," *Journal of Medical Education*, July 1973, pp. 630–635.

Chapter Two

1. Associated Press story, December 18, 1976.
2. "Nominal and Verbal Styles: Some Affective Consequences" (Paper delivered before the Midwest Modern Language Association, 1975).
3. The source of the grade distributions in San Antonio is the pamphlet *College Bound Students (1968–1975)*, Research & Development Department, San Antonio Independent

School District, San Antonio, Texas (November 1975), p. 10.

Chapter Three

1.   *Arizona Daily Star,* October 29, 1976, Section B, p. 1.

Chapter Four

1.   C. K. Hyder, *George Lyman Kittredge, Teacher and Scholar* (Lawrence, Kansas: University of Kansas Press, 1962), p. 120.
2.   George Lyman Kittredge and F. E. Farley, *An Advanced English Grammar* (Boston: Ginn, 1913), p. xiv.
3.   W. Nelson Francis, "Revolution in Grammar," *Quarterly Journal of Speech,* October 1954, p. 300.
4.   *Ibid.,* p. 299.
5.   Leonard Bloomfield, *Language* (New York: Henry Holt, 1933), p. 22.
6.   Robert Pooley, *Grammar and Usage in Textbooks on English* (Madison, Wisconsin: University of Wisconsin, 1933), p. 12.
7.   *Ibid.,* pp. 36–37.
8.   C. C. Fries, *American English Grammar* (New York: Appleton-Century, 1940), pp. 2–3.
9.   George Campbell, *The Philosophy of Rhetoric,* ed. Lloyd F. Bitzer (Carbondale, Illinois: Southern Illinois University Press, 1963), pp. 139–140.
10. Hugh Blair, *Lectures on Rhetoric and Belles Lettres,* ed. Harold Harding (Carbondale, Illinois: Southern Illinois University Press, 1965), I, p. 179.
11. Kittredge and Farley, *op. cit.,* p. xvi. Writers of textbooks used by American Victorians found it easy to accept the idea that usage creates and governs "the rules." Three examples: Language "assumes any and every form which those who make use of it choose to give it. We are, therefore, as *rational* and *practical* grammarians, compelled to

submit to the necessity of the case; to take the language as it *is*, and not as it *should be*, and bow to custom" (Samuel Kirkham, *English Grammar* [Rochester, N.Y.: William Alling, 1845], p. 18). G. P. Quackenbos wrote that "it is evident that usage is the only standard both of speaking and writing; that it is the highest tribunal to which, in cases of grammatical controversy, we can appeal" (*Advanced Course of Composition and Rhetoric* [New York: Appleton, 1882], p. 274). Adams Sherman Hill stated that "grammarians and lexicographers have no authority not derived from good use" (*The Principles of Rhetoric* [New York: American Book Co., 1895], p. 17).

12. Benjamin Lee Whorf, "Linguistics as an Exact Science," *Language, Thought, and Reality,* ed. John B. Carroll (Cambridge, Massachusetts: MIT Press, 1956), p. 221.

13. Paul Roberts, *Understanding English* (New York: Harper, 1958), p. 143.

14. James B. McMillan, "A Philosophy of Language," *College English*, April 1948, p. 390.

15. Resolution passed by the National Council of Teachers of English, November 22, 1951, at the general business meeting. Quoted by C. C. Fries, "Advances in Linguistics," *College English*, October 1961, p. 36, n. 7.

16. Campbell, *op. cit.*, p. 259.

17. Bloomfield, *op. cit.*, pp. 20–22.

18. NCTE Commission on the English Curriculum, *The English Language Arts* (New York: Appleton-Century-Crofts, 1952), pp. 275–277. Of the Pentalogue, this volume states, "In the last half century linguists who have devoted themselves to the study of the English language have evolved five basic concepts which are, or should be, the foundation of the current attitude toward any teaching of the English language today" (p. 274).

19. Sheridan Baker, "The Error of *Ain't*," *College English*, November 1964, p. 100.

20. J. H. Gardiner, G. L. Kittredge, and S. L. Arnold, *Manual of Composition and Rhetoric* (Boston: Ginn, 1907), p. 346.

21. Observations on the *Third* are collected in *Dictionaries and That Dictionary*, eds. James Sledd and Wilma Ebbitt (Glenview, Illinois: Scott, Foresman, 1962).

22. Philip Gove, "Linguistic Advances and Lexicography," *Ibid.*, pp. 65–74.

23. "A New Field Guide to Word Watching" (Springfield, Massachusetts: G. and C. Merriam, 1963). Unpaged pamphlet.

24. Jacques Barzun, "What is A Dictionary?" *American Scholar*, 32 (1963): 176.

25. W. Nelson Francis, "Language and Linguistics in the English Program," *College English*, October 1964, pp. 14–15.

26. James Sledd, "New and Newer Grammars of English: Remarks on Their Present Status," *Illinois English Bulletin*, May 1964, p. 6.

27. "Cultural Lag and Reviewers of *Webster III*," *AAUP Bulletin*, December 1963, p. 365. It is necessary to document this point. Barzun's second paragraph reads in full as follows: "All this is gratifying. For it shows that despite the many signs of linguistic indifference in daily life, some people at least still *feel strongly about language* and can be roused to battle about it. The *debate* has not been confined to print, and it is not over; *it* is very much alive in living rooms, students' rooms, editorial rooms. When *it* came up as a subject of interest at a meeting of the board of the *American Scholar*, everyone present felt that *its* importance warranted notice from one of us, and I was delegated to express the board's 'position.' This was extraordinary, for more than one reason. Never in my experience has the Editorial Board desired to reach a position; it respects without effort the individuality of each member and contributor, and it expects and relishes diversity. What is even more remarkable, none of those present had given the new dictionary more than a casual glance, yet each

one felt that he knew how he stood on the *issue* that the work presented to the public" (p. 176, *italics added*). Dykema reduces this to: "In the Spring 1963, *American Scholar* Jacques Barzun asserts that in condemning the dictionary he is expressing the position of the editorial board of that magazine. He confesses, however, that 'none of those present [at the meeting of the board] had given the new dictionary more than a casual glance. . . .' To condemn a book of nearly three thousand three-column pages on the basis of a 'casual glance' hardly seems to demonstrate the 'judicial tolerance and the scholarly temper' (p. 176) which Mr. Barzun claims for his editorial board" (p. 365). It is clear from Barzun's paragraph that he was not delegated to "condemn" the dictionary but to express the board's "position" on the debate about language with (by implication) special reference to the dictionary. Further, by omitting the last part of Barzun's final sentence, Dykema makes it appear that the board had already condemned the dictionary when actually each member simply "knew how he stood on the *issue* that the work presented to the public" (*italics added*).

28. Kenneth Wilson, "The Portable Liberator," *CEA Critic*, March 1964, p. 1.

29. Richard Martin, "The Word Watchers," *Wall Street Journal*, November 28, 1973, p. 1.

30. *Students' Right to Their Own Language*, Conference on College Composition and Communication (Fall 1974).

31. NCTE news release, November 28, 1976.

32. *College English*, February 1976, p. 631.

33. NCTE news release, November 28, 1976.

34. *College English*, February 1976, p. 628.

35. National Assessment of Educational Progress, *Writing Mechanics, 1969–1974: A Capsule Description of Changes in Writing Mechanics*, Writing Report No. 05-W-01 (October 1975), p. 43.

36. Thomas J. Farrell, "Literacy, the Basics, and All That Jazz," *College English,* January 1977, p. 459.
37. Hans Guth, "Forward to Basics: Developing the Language Potential," *Kansas English,* December 1976, p. 9.
38. George Nash, "Who's Minding Freshman English at U.T. Austin?" *College English,* October 1976, p. 127.
39. *Ibid.,* pp. 129–130.

Chapter Five

1. Ambrose Bierce, *Collected Writings of Ambrose Bierce* (New York: Citadel Press, 1946), p. 251.
2. Quoted in Morris Kline, *Why Johnny Can't Add: The Failure of the New Math* (New York: St. Martin's, 1973), p. 110.
3. Charlton Laird, *A Writer's Handbook* (Boston: Ginn, 1964), pp. 113–114.
4. Dwight Bolinger, *Aspects of Language* (New York: Harcourt, Brace and World, 1968), pp. 116–117.
5. Wayne O'Neil, from whom we borrowed the sentence, diagrams it using a transformational "tree graph":

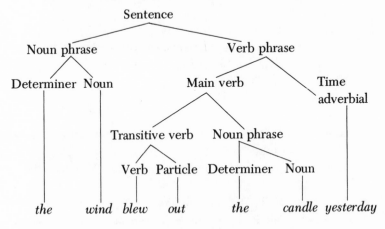

From *Kernels and Transformations: A Modern Grammar of English* (New York: McGraw-Hill, 1965), p. 17.

6. See Francis Christensen, *Notes Toward A New Rhetoric* (New York: Harper and Row, 1967).

7. L. M. Myers, *Guide to American English* (Englewood Cliffs, New Jersey: Prentice-Hall, 1968), p. 433.

8. Stephen Koch, "Intrigue and the Wringing of Hands," *World*, August 28, 1973, p. 58.

Chapter Six

1. Clyde Hyder, *George Lyman Kittredge* (Lawrence, Kansas: University of Kansas Press, 1962), p. 67.

2. Quoted in Sir Ernest Gowers, *Plain Words: Their ABC* (New York: Knopf, 1962), pp. 46–47.

3. Associated Press story, January 27, 1977.

4. *Tract No. 1, Society for Pure English* (London: Oxford University Press, 1919) pp. 6–7.

5. *Ibid.,* p. 9.

6. Jacques Barzun, "The Retort Circumstantial," *American Scholar*, 20 (Summer 1951) 293.

7. Orwell, *op. cit.,* 4:136.

8. *Bulletin of The Council for Basic Education,* February 1969, pp. 1–4.

9. *Ibid.,* November 1969, pp. 9–10.

10. Samuel Kirkham, *English Grammar* (Rochester, New York: William Alling, 1845), p. 15.

11. Thomas Pyles, *The Origins and Development of the English Language* (New York: Harcourt, Brace and World, 1964), p. 17.

12. Allen W. Read, "Is American English Deteriorating?" *Word Study*, October 1965, p. 1.

13. George Orwell, *1984* (London: Secker and Warburg, 1951), pp. 15–16.

14. Robert A. Hall, "Telling the Truth," *The Role of the Dictionary*, ed. Philip B. Gove (Indianapolis: Bobbs-Merrill, 1967), p. 27. Hall's comments were originally published in

the scholarly journal *Quarterly Journal of Speech*, December 1962, p. 435.

15. V. S. Naipaul, "What's Wrong With Being a Snob?" *Saturday Evening Post*, June 3, 1967, p. 18.

16. "Black Nonsense," *The Crisis*, April–May 1971, p. 78.

17. Ralph Waldo Emerson, from his *Journals* (June 24, 1840), in *Selected Prose and Poetry*, ed. Reginald Cook (New York: Holt, Rinehart and Winston, 1960), p. 475.

18. Wilbur Samuel Howell, "Renaissance Rhetoric and Modern Rhetoric: A Study in Change," *The Province of Rhetoric*, eds. Joseph Schwartz and John Rycenga (New York: Ronald Press, 1965), p. 299.

19. Aristotle, *Nicomachean Ethics*, trans. W. D. Ross (London: Oxford University Press, 1942), i. 3. 1094b13–28.

20. G. K. Chesterton, *Robert Browning* (New York: Macmillan, 1903), p. 31.